SOCIAL DREAMING
@ WORK

W. Gordon Lawrence

SOCIAL DREAMING
@ WORK

edited by

W. Gordon Lawrence

Introduction by

David Armstrong

London
KARNAC BOOKS

First published in 1998 by
H. Karnac (Books) Ltd.
58 Gloucester Road
London SW7 4QY

British Library Cataloguing in Publication Data

A C.I.P. record for this book is available from the British Library.

ISBN 1 85575 209 3

Edited, designed, and produced by Communication Crafts

Printed in Great Britain by BPCC Wheatons Ltd, Exeter

10 9 8 7 6 5 4 3 2 1

In Memory of Sam Lawrence,
3rd July, 1993 to 3rd December, 1996

From the poets of all ages and from the depths of their souls this tremendous vision of the flowing away of life like water has wrung bitter cries—from Pindar's "dream of a shadow," to Calderón's "life is a dream" and Shakespeare's "we are such stuff as dreams are made on," this last a yet more tragic sentence than Calderón's, for whereas the Castilian only declares that our life is a dream, but not that we ourselves are the dreamers of it, the Englishman makes *ourselves a dream, a dream that dreams.*

Miguel de Unamuno, *Tragic Sense of Life,*
1954, p. 39 [italics added]

ACKNOWLEDGEMENTS

I am grateful to the following for permission to reprint: to The Grubb Institute, London, for David Armstrong, "Thinking Aloud: Contributions to Three Dialogues" (1991); to the Systems-Centered Press, Philadelphia, PA, *SCT Journal: Systems-Centered Theory and Practice*, Vol. 2 (August 1997), pp. 18–22, for Thomas Michael, "Does that Dream Have a Subgroup: The Uses of Dreams on Systems-Centered Theory"; to the editor and publisher of *Free Associations*, Vol. 2, Part 2 (1991, No. 22), pp. 259–294, for W. Gordon Lawrence, "Won from the Void and Formless Infinite: Experiences of Social Dreaming". For excerpts from the following two articles, I acknowledge: the editor and publisher of *Group Analysis*, Vol. 27 (No. 3, 1994), pp. 319–328, for Herbert Hahn, "Dreaming to Learn: Pathways to Rediscovery"; and the editor (M. A. Mattoon) and publisher of *Open Questions in Analytical Psychology: Proceedings of the Thirteenth International Congress for Analytical Psychology*, Daimon, Einsiedeln, for Peter Tatham and Helen Morgan, "The Social Dreaming Matrix" (1997).

Finally, I am especially grateful to the hundreds of people, in various parts of the world, who have taken part in social dreaming matrices. It is they who have given flesh to an idea that is always in a process of being formulated, but becomes that much more rich on each occasion. To them I owe an enormous debt.

CONTENTS

ACKNOWLEDGEMENTS   vii

ABOUT THE CONTRIBUTORS   xi

INTRODUCTION
        David Armstrong   xvii

Prologue
        W. Gordon Lawrence   1

1   "Won from the void and formless infinite":
    experiences of social dreaming
        W. Gordon Lawrence   9

2   Dreaming to learn: pathways to rediscovery
        Herbert Hahn   43

3   Vision in organizational life
        Kenneth Eisold   49

4   The use of dreams in systems-centred theory
     Thomas A. Michael   59

5   The social dreaming matrix
     Peter Tatham and Helen Morgan   69

6   After Shakespeare—the language of social dreaming
     Francis Oeser   75

7   Thinking aloud: contributions to three dialogues
     David Armstrong   91

8   Creating new cultures:
     the contribution of social dreaming
     Thomas A. Michael   107

9   Social dreaming as a tool of consultancy
     and action research
     W. Gordon Lawrence   123

10   Simultaneity and parallel process:
     an on-line applied social dreaming matrix
     Marc Maltz and E. Martin Walker   141

11   Social dreaming @ work
     W. Gordon Lawrence, Marc Maltz,
     and E. Martin Walker   169

REFERENCES   183

INDEX   189

ABOUT THE CONTRIBUTORS

David Armstrong is Senior Consultant at the Tavistock Consultancy Service of the Tavistock Centre, London, and a professional associate of The Grubb Institute. He trained as a psychologist at Cambridge University and at the Tavistock Institute of Human Relations, where he was involved in action research programmes on management innovation and the impact of automation on organizational structure. He is a member of the International Society for the Psychoanalytic Study of Organizations and has published widely. His consultancy work has been with a wide variety of public and private sector organizations. His approach to consultancy draws on systemic and psychoanalytic thinking, while seeking to keep the focus on the clients' experience of their organization and the dilemmas, tensions, and challenges presented to them in their roles.

Kenneth Eisold is a practising psychoanalyst and organizational consultant. He is Director of the Organizational Programme at the William Alanson White Institute, where he also teaches and supervises. He is past Director of the A. K. Rice Institute's National Conference and an Institute Fellow. In addition to his doctorate in Clinical Psychology and his certificate in Psychoanalysis, he holds a doctorate in English and Comparative Literature. His publications, several of which have been published in the *International Journal of Psycho-Analysis*, have focused recently on the psychodynamics of psychoanalytic institutions. They have also dealt with such diverse topics as dreams, literature and psychoanalysis, theories of group behaviour, and authority. He is an Associate Editor of *Contemporary Psychoanalysis*.

Herbert Hahn, a Chartered Psychologist and a full member of the British Association of Psychotherapists and Group Psychotherapists, was a co-founder and the first Chairman of the Severnside Institute of Psychotherapy. He was a staff member of the Tavistock Institute of Human Relations and a Senior Faculty Member of the European School of Management Studies. He has worked in Management Selection and Professional and Executive Career Development. Currently, he specializes in role consultation for chief executives, supervision of other consultants, and facilitation of managers and senior staff groups. He is also a Special Lecturer in Organisational Development on the MSc course in Occupational Psychology at Bristol University. His interest in social dreaming emerged from his training in Group Relations at the Tavistock, and has been sharpened and deepened by learning at first hand from Gordon Lawrence. He has facilitated and co-facilitated several social dreaming matrices in England and South Africa.

W. Gordon Lawrence is currently Visiting Professor of Organizational Behaviour, Cranfield University, Bedford, and Visiting Fellow, School of Management, Lancaster University. He is a Fellow of the Australian Institute of Social Analysis, a Managing Partner of Symbiont Technologies LLC, New York and London, and also a director of IMAGO East-West and Symbiont Ventures, London. He worked at the Tavistock Institute of Human Relations for eleven years, where he was joint-director of the Institute's Group Relations Programme. He has published extensively in books and journals over the years and edited *Exploring Individual and Organizational Boundaries* (1979) and *Roots in a Northern Landscape* (1996a). His poems appear in Ian Olson's, *No Other Place* (1995).

Marc Maltz is a graduate of the Organizational Development and Consultancy Programme at the William Alanson White Institute (WAWI) of Psychiatry, Psychoanalysis and Psychology, New York. He holds a Masters in Business Administration, a Master of Arts in History, and post-graduate certificates from MIT's Executive Programme in Technology and The Wharton School's Executive Programme in Finance. He is currently a Faculty member of the WAWI's programme in Organizational Consultation. He is a member of the A. K. Rice Institute's Center for the Study of Groups and Social Systems and the New York Center, the International Society for the Study of Organizations, and the Organizational Development Network. His more recent publications focus on further defining and consulting to organizations. He is a Principal and founder of TRIAD Consulting Group, LLC and a Managing Partner of Symbiont Technologies, LLC. He previously held executive positions at AT&T, Westinghouse Electric Company, NYNEX Corporation, and Music Mining Co., Inc. He specializes in individual role and organizational development. A group process and systems consultant, he works with individuals and teams to balance the dynamics experienced in the workplace with understanding and achieving team and business objectives.

Tom Michael is Associate Professor in the Department of Management and MIS at Rowan University, New Jersey, where he teaches organizational behaviour, organizational change and development, and strategic planning. He is a member of the International Society for the Psychoanalytic Study of Organization, the A. K. Rice Institute, and the Systems-Centered Theory Institute. He is an ordained minister in the Presbyterian Church in the United States. In addition to his interest in social dreaming applications, he has done research and consulting in career and organizational development, conflict resolution, and future-research planning.

Helen Morgan is a Full Member of the Jungian Analytic Section of the British Association of Psychotherapists. She is currently in private practice working as a psychotherapist, a trainer, and a consultant to organizations. Her background is in mental health work, and she has worked in therapeutic communities with both adolescents and adults. Her publications and papers include: *A*

Psychodynamic Perspective on Group Process (1996, co-written with Kerry Thomas), "Between Fear and Blindness—The White Therapist and the Black Patient" (1998a), and "Looking for the Crevices: Consultation in the Mental Health Service" (1998b).

Francis Oeser studied architecture, journalism, and town and regional planning at Melbourne University, and later Shakespeare Studies at the Shakespeare Institute, Stratford-upon-Avon (Birmingham University). A poet and musician, he was born in St. Andrews (Scotland) and grew up and was educated in Australia and now lives in London and Aegina (Greece). He has published ten books of poetry since 1983. In 1997, he was awarded two first prizes: for a libretto called "Islands" (music by Constantinos Lignos), which he performed in Greece in 1996, and for an opera libretto called "Persephone" (sets by Mark Strizic). His professional work as an architect/planner and teacher and his experience at a Leicester Conference and FIIS conferences in Evry (France) were significances in his journey towards social dreaming. He has experienced "being a stranger in a strange land"; he wants to share something of the enrichment of such "displacement" that, for instance, a waking person dealing with dream material can experience.

Peter Tatham worked for fifteen years in general practice and as a family practitioner before retraining as an analyst at the C.G. Jung Institute in Zurich. Since returning to England in 1978, he has maintained a private analytic practice, outside London. During that time, he has also lectured and taught widely on Jungian subjects. His book *The Makings of Maleness* was published in 1992. He first became interested in social dreaming in 1994 and has since used it in a variety of settings. He is currently setting up an ongoing research project to meet monthly over the course of a year, entitled: "Dreaming a Millennium".

Edward Martin Walker, PhD, lived in Argentina, Brazil, Chile, Denmark, India, Nepal, Switzerland, and the United States prior to the age of 24. Following undergraduate degrees in Management, Religion, and Psychology at New York University, he received a doctorate from the City University of New York with a dissertation applying Wilfred Bion's group psychoanalytic theories to cultural identity and inter-group relations. He is a candidate at the William Alanson White Institute in New York and is practising psychology in medical rehabilitation and the final stages of life. Currently, he is a Managing Partner of Symbiont Technologies LLC, New York. As a Fulbright Scholar (Mexico), he examined the psychosocial aspects of the North American Free Trade Agreement; his principal focus on organizations is on shadow phenomena and dreaming.

INTRODUCTION

David Armstrong

"Social dreaming" is the name given to a method of working with dreams that are shared and associated to within a gathering of people, coming together for this purpose. Its immediate origins date back to the early 1980s. At that time, Gordon Lawrence was on the scientific staff of the Tavistock Institute of Human Relations. He was a core member of the Institute's Group Relations Programme, within which he had developed a distinctive approach centring around the concept of "relatedness"—that is, the ways in which individual experience and behaviour reflects and is structured by conscious and unconscious constructs of the group or organization in the mind.

As a consultant in group relations conferences, Lawrence was familiar with occasions when a group member would recount a dream that appeared to speak to the experience of others. However, his own experience of recounting dreams in psychoanalytic sessions made him cautious in approaching this material. At the same time he was also familiar, from reading, travel, and conversations, with other perspectives on dreaming and its significance in social and cultural life: as prophecy, fortune-telling, access to a good or a bad spirit, vision. These perspectives, often associated with accounts of dreaming offered by so-called "primitive" peoples, seemed to point to a different kind of relation between the dream and the dreamer to that explored in psychoanalysis: a relation not so much between different aspects, or experiences, of the self as between the self and the "Other", where the dreamer, as it were, gives voice to the dream that is *in* him or her but not just *of* him or her.

Lawrence has described these as "two facts held in my mind. . . . I vaguely felt there had to be a connection between the two, but it was beyond me" (Lawrence, 1989). The link came by chance when Lawrence followed up a reference to a book by Charlotte Beradt (1968) called *The Third Reich of Dreams*, in which the author recounts hundreds of dreams of Germans collected between 1933 and 1939. These multiple dreams had a characteristic quality in that the link between dream image and reality often appeared to lie close to the surface of the dream. Taken together, they could be seen as rehearsing, presenting, and foreshadowing political events and people's responses to and constructions of these events in ways that were mutually illuminating.

If dreams had this potential to disclose and illuminate social and political realities, might there not be ways in which this could be put to work and mobilized in the service of understanding? Together with Patricia Daniel, a colleague at the Tavistock, Lawrence framed the idea of having "a group of people who would dream socially". In 1982 the first experiment in "social dreaming" was mounted and called simply "A Project in Social Dreaming and Creativity". It ran over eight weeks, made up of weekly sessions of one and a half hours, with thirteen members of varied professional backgrounds, most of whom were familiar with the Tavistock tradition of group study. The sessions were named as a "Social Dreaming Matrix", where matrix had the meaning of "a place out of which something grows". (The use of this term was also designed to avoid the associations that would have clustered around the concept of "group". To borrow a usage of Wilfred Bion's, what was needed was an "unsaturated" term, whose meaning was to be found in and from the experience generated in such a "place", without, as far as possible, importing other, more familiar frames of reference.)

Within these sessions, members were invited to share and associate to their dreams and to explore their possible social meanings. It was this task that focused the work, without regard to group processes, attention to which would have played into defences.

For six years nothing further happened. At that time Lawrence had left the Tavistock and was unsure how to take things further. Then in 1988 he was invited to design a programme for therapists and organizational consultants working in Israel and concerned with issues of leadership and innovation. The programme was to be experimental and germane to the *métier* of its members. Lawrence decided that this was an opportunity to try the social dreaming matrix again and build a programme around it.

Since that second venture, the idea of social dreaming has caught the imagination. Further programmes have been held in Germany, Sweden, the United Kingdom, Belgium, India, Australia, and the United States. Adaptations of the method have been developed and used in a variety of other professional and organizational contexts. While these programmes have varied in their particular focus, range of membership, and application, they have all retained at their core the experience of the social dreaming matrix: a gathering of participants committed to sharing their dreams.

Borrowing, again, from a formulation of Bion's, one might think of this name, "social dreaming matrix", as binding "a constant conjunction . . . of certain experiences, facts or events . . . agglomerated, articulated or integrated in time" (Bion, 1992, pp. 13–14) the meaning of which remains to be discovered. Naming serves as a prelude to meaning. It denotes an area for exploration.

The social dreaming matrix as I experience it acts as a "container" within which this human potential can be brought into focus and put to work, and offered to our curiosity about the meaning and significance of the implicate order, to echo David Bohm (1980), of our world.

The contributions that Lawrence has brought together in this book are severally and together a venture in such an exploration. The conjunctions that they are seeking to probe are the experiences present and presented through the communication of dreams within a social context. This context is both actual—people gathered together in a contained space—and virtual, in the sense that this space is defined in relation to some determined boundary—of citizenship, organization, profession, or social attachment—that is held in the mind. It is within this social context or space that the phenomena of social dreaming unfold.

The conjunctions that recur and proliferate within this space, illustrated in this book, concern, for example, the sequencing of dream material offered by members; the interplay of imagery; the patterning of association both to and between dreams; the ways in which dreams appear to converse with each other; most strangely perhaps, the experience of sometimes seeming to hear from another the "dream" that one could not remember oneself.

What links such experiences together might be described, to return to a point made earlier, as the sense of the dream as "Other": a kind of visitation, something wider than a personal construct, which is giving voice to an experience that is not of oneself alone.

I suggest that more generally a dream can be seen as a communication both from and into a certain context or "mental space" (Young, 1994). By "mental space" I understand a container for emotional experience. The dream is a registration of emotional experience within that space, itself a prelude to thought. The boundaries of mental space are, however, not fixed coordinates. Or, to put it another way, there is no privileged location for emotional experience: it is not always and perhaps is not ever the property of the individual alone. In psychoanalytic work, for example, as I understand it, the emotional experience that is the focus of exploration is not simply that of the patient. Rather, it is the experience of the analytic couple—analyst and analysand—of what passes or passages between them. A dream communicated in a psychoanalytic session has meaning, gives voice to, or registers emotional experience within just this mental space: the space of the analytic encounter. From this point of view, the psychoanalytic account of dreams and dreaming is not so much a universal, generalizable theory as an account and theory of the dream in a specific context, a context suffused with the phenomena of transference and countertransference.

What Lawrence has discovered or rediscovered in the social dreaming matrix is another context or contexts for dreaming, in which the emotional experience on which our capacity for dreaming, for entertaining dream thoughts, works is not that of the pair but that of the *many*: group, society, tribe, collective, race, species. Within this or these contexts, the meanings of the dream and dreaming spread out to capture and formulate echoes-of-the-thoughts-that-are-there, in the space between the "many-in-mind".

SOCIAL DREAMING
@ WORK

Prologue

W. Gordon Lawrence

his collection of essays could well have the subtitle "Further Explorations in Social Dreaming", because the concept of *social dreaming* is in an emergent state, a process of becoming. They can be seen as notes towards a theory of social dreaming which is not completed, and may never be—one that concentrates on free association and amplification as methods of scientific investigation, with a holistic approach to the sources, contents, and associations of dreams.

In a newsletter of the Indian Society of Applied Behavioural Studies, Gouranga Chattopadhyay wrote to the effect that most of the *Upanishads* states, of which we are all a part, form a boundary-less cosmos called *Paramatman, Atman,* or *Brahman* and that this is substantiated by contemporary quantum mechanics. Human beings create boundaries to explain what they perceive as well as to defend themselves from the anxiety of the terror of living in a boundary-less, infinite world. But dreams connect us fundamentally to the roots of life in a world governed by quantum mechanics, in which life and matter cannot be differentiated absolutely.

Dreams themselves are boundary-less. They range across time and space. They are an emotional experience presented through metaphors. They are also a synthesis that has the truth embedded in the dream if we can discern its meaning by amplification. Dreams have been, we can assume, a feature of human life since man first appeared in the world through the process of evolution—and, indeed, my argument is that dreaming/dream-work is essential for the process of evolution.

Since Freud (1900), dreams and dreaming have been part of the scientific project of psychoanalysis and as such were seen in terms of "interpretation". Dreams were subject to causal analysis, and terms such as "concretization", "censor", "displacement", and "condensation" were developed to explain the processes involved in dreaming and not remembering dreams. It was a monumental effort to render dreams as a suitable vehicle for scientific analysis and to make them amenable for use in psychoanalysis.

There is a very real sense, however, in which dreams cannot be "interpreted" using the conscious, rational mind exclusively. Once the dream is made into an object (and the moment it is spoken it becomes so), it loses its quintessential, existential subjectivity and, inevitably, becomes distorted, with its potential, original meaning liable to obliteration. The dream is a biological necessity and "a natural phenomenon that cannot be produced by conscious will" (Meier, 1987, p. 106), and, as such, it can only "be observed and expressed with psychic means" (p. 5). We need a methodology that is congruent with unconscious processes, does not betray them, and does not seek refuge in conscious, unwittingly defensive, boundary-bound, reductionist ratiocination.

The dream is, as I understand it, the essential transaction between the inner, unconscious, infinite world of the psyche and the external world of the conscious, finite experiences of the "I" and the "Other". The dream is a parallel, anticipatory state of our being-in-the-world. By this I mean that genetic information (transmitted by DNA)—sparked by emotional experiences of sensory data experienced in the outside environment—is processed by dreaming, in part, to anticipate the searching for analogous experiences in waking life. Dreaming is a contextual process, conducted by the total, living entity in relation to the eco-space in which the entity exists. By "total, living entity", I mean consciousness, the unconscious, DNA, intelligence, will, mind, etc., *plus* the unknown factor that arises from the existence of more than the sum of the parts. If you will, out of the interaction of the sum of the finite elements of being there is invoked a process that belongs to the domain of dreaming and is "Won from the void and formless infinite", to quote Bion (1965, p. 151). Dreaming is the expression of the symbiotic urge of the psyche to be in a mutual state of existence with its eco-space, or its environment. Neither could exist, nor have being, without the other. Dreaming can be conceived of as the "wave" function of the psyche that continues without ceasing, occasionally to be realized in a dream as a "particle" that is remembered by the "I" as a whole dream, or as a fragment.

Dreaming is essential to evolution. In the Archean period, some 3.6 thousand million (aeons) ago, the Earth emerged as a living organism through cynobacteria. It was covered in huge lakes, or swathes, of cynobacteria, which had emerged from matter by forming in eddies and whirlpools. Cynobacteria used their solid state of matter to store and transmit the message of existence to their descendants—bacteria can readily exchange information encoded in chains of nucleic acids called plasmids. From these beginnings, all subsequent life emerged. My working hypothesis is that cynobacteria, and subsequent bacteria, were involved in a form of "proto-dreaming" as a method of processing information. All living entities exist in an ecological system, and forces from outside cause them to evolve. The proto-dreaming, and subsequent dreaming, are the methods by which total, living entities adapt to the forces from outside by anticipating through the flexibility of "mental space" (Young, 1994) what can be learned from just being and existing in the eco-space.

In the long process of evolution, I am postulating that in the beginning was dreaming: then came the word. But, irrespective of whether my conjectures have any validity, the fact is that dreaming has been an essential part of human life since the beginning of mankind. Social dreaming attempts to make dreaming ordinary and, by seeing it as a holistic project, to rescue it from the reductionist, specialist frameworks that are used to interpret dreams.

A number of approaches to an understanding of social dreaming are contained herein. The first chapter sets the scene for an exploration of social dreaming. It is a statement of what was thought out a few years ago, but which is always in a process of revision. Herbert Hahn then describes the surprise of learning from social dreaming in an educational setting, which led to the experience of openness in unprecedented ways. Kenneth Eisold writes of the place and necessity of vision in organizational life. Sometimes vision can be an expression of "no-dream", sometimes not. If vision arises from no-dream, how valuable is it? Thomas Michael used dreams in a group and shows how they can be mobilized around, and he points to the connection between dream and action. The distinction between "group" and "matrix" takes on a new meaning. Peter Tatham and Helen Morgan describe how social dreaming was responsible for a sense of wholeness and connection emerging at a professional meeting that had previously had a social climate characterized by divisive "politics". Francis Oeser writes of the metaphors that suffuse dreaming and relates these as developed in a social dreaming matrix to the work of Shakespeare. David Armstrong gives substance to the idea that all dreamers are thinkers by showing that "Thinking 2" and the nature of the thought processes that inform dreaming come together in a vivid and striking way.

In the second of his chapters in this collection, Thomas Michael introduces the theme of dreaming in organizational life, indicating ways in which this can be furthered. An "organization" refers to any institution such as a company, a religious order, a hospital, a prison, an army, and so forth. The remaining chapters by Marc Maltz, Martin Walker, and myself attempt to lodge social dreaming firmly in the world of the organization.

The unexpected result of social dreaming arises from the primary task, or purpose, that gives an emergent quality to a social dreaming matrix—that is, to discover social meanings. In both face-to-face configurations and on-line on the Internet, the result is the uncovering of social meaning to *all* events, achieved through free association and amplification. While free association mobilizes linear thinking, amplification stays with the dream and produces new meanings and insights. This is an additional feature of action research and consultancy, which, up to now, have been constrained by the demands of logic that organizational thinking involves. The unconscious elements of organizations have been reduced to identifying the social systems of defence against anxieties. In many ways, this has become banalized as a ready-made "interpretation", explaining away the subtleties of organizational life in terms of Oedipus.

I take the distinction from Bion where he writes that one can view group life from two vertices, that of "Oedipus" and that of "sphinx". He writes,

> I am impressed, as a practising psycho-analyst, by the fact that the psycho-analytic approach, through the individual, and the approach these papers describe, through the group, are dealing with different facets of the same phenomenon. The two methods provide the practitioner with a rudimentary binocular vision. The observations tend to fall into two categories, whose affinity is shown by phenomena, which, when examined by one method, centre on the Oedipal situation, related to the pairing group, and, when examined by the other, centre on the sphinx, related to problems of knowledge and scientific method. [Bion, 1961, p. 8]

As a psychoanalytically orientated organization consultant, I focus on "sphinx" while holding "Oedipus" in mind. The latter I regard as a proper business of the analyst and the analysand in the classic psychoanalytic encounter. In organizational work I focus primarily on the nature of the thinking that role-holders are evincing and not on the psychopathology of the individual in roles within it. The connection between dream-work and thinking is straightforward, though it is difficult to acknowledge.

Now, through social dreaming, we can begin to see organizations in a new light, because a more complete conceptualization becomes possible. All organizations are the outcome of thinking and thought. Imagine what would happen if everyone turned up at Shell International, say, having forgotten what they were there to do! As it is, organizational consultancy tends to focus on two dimensions of the thinking in an organization. There is, first, *the life and work of the organization as it is experienced as a process*. This includes all the dimensions and features of organizational life: the managerial structure, the purpose and its meaning, the interrelationship of units or departments on each other, the production system, the human resource management, and, in general, the meaning of the organization as a continual process in the minds of the role-holders in both its conscious and unconscious senses. This is the material on which the consultant is invited to work.

Often, however, consultants are called upon to work on the planning of the future of the organization. So we can identify a second feature of organizational life: *the life and work of the organization as it is in the process of becoming*. This is the emergent quality of organizations which the role-holders bring into being. While planning calls for divergent thinking on the part of the organizational members and the consultant, it is often reduced to an exercise in predicting the future, seeing what the organizational members (usually the management) want their future to look like, and devising ways of making sure that the future comes out that way. All these are very shaky premises.

Divergent, creative thinking is replaced, in this case, by what is felt to be sure and certain logical, linear thinking—but who can predict the future as an arrow of time flying straight to its target? We live and work in an uncertain environment, characterized by turbulence. The causal relationships, identified by Isaac Newton, have been expanded to include the ideas of randomness and unpredictability. As Einstein once said: "The Universe is not only queerer than we suppose. It is queerer than we can suppose." All planning ventures have to take this "queerness" into consideration as the world becomes more of a "global village", characterized by instant communication through acoustic space (see chapter eleven) by means of information technology. We no longer live exclusively in Euclidean space. Unknown factors arise from the interaction of the unknown qualities of features and events in the environment. One method of anticipating the future is to write scenarios of different futures so that planning is able to make use of contingencies as circumstances change—as they surely will.

There is another dimension to organizational life which has hitherto never been tapped directly and made use of in the process of planning: *the life and work of the organization as it is in the process of being dreamt*. The working hypothesis that Maltz, Walker, and I put forward begins to grapple with this third dimension, seeing it as a parallel process and as a source of simultaneity.

We can now imagine an organization as being organized around these three features, which together compose its context (see Figure 1). The substantive thinking of the organization lies between these dimensions. Hitherto, organizational consultancy has taken only the first two dimensions into account. Now we are finding methods for making use of what has until now been a hidden, unknown dimension—the third dimension.

Bion (1992) wrote:

> The failure of dream-work and the consequent lack of availability of experience of external or internal psychic reality gives rise to the peculiar state of the psychotic who seems to have a contact with reality but is able to make singularly little use of it either for learning by experience or for immediate consumption. [p. 45]

Psychotic thinking is based on a hatred of reality and the overarching wish to "split off" the good from the bad, to make the understanding of living simple by avoiding complexity and ambiguity. Often, we find that heads of organizations are prone to psychotic thinking because of the unconscious forces at work in an organization (Lawrence, 1995a, 1995b). While contact with reality is not dependent on dreaming, what is critical is accessibility to the personality of the material derived from this contact, which is

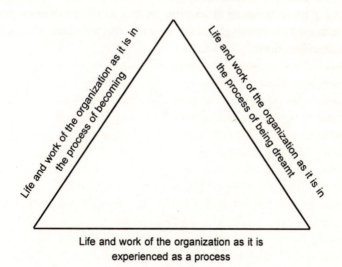

Life and work of the organization as it is
experienced as a process

FIGURE 1   Application of Social Dreaming to the Organization

dependent on dream-work. As I understand it, the psychotic not having access to the nature of dream material is always engaged in having a no-dream—that is, a hallucination. One wonders how many role-holders in organizations are subject to leadership that has no access to their dream material in any form, who are always engaged in the no-dream. It is for this reason that I am suspicious of the idea of vision, particularly vision that has had no contact with dream-work. How many of us are engaged in the life and work of an organization and find ourselves living out the no-dream, the hallucination, of the leadership? I am reminded of the *dénouement* to the short story, "The Circular Ruins" contained in *Ficciones* by Jorge Luis Borges (1993), which ends with the protagonist and dreamer walking towards the sheets of flame and recognizing, "With relief, with humiliation, with terror, he understood that he was also an illusion, that someone else was dreaming him".

For some time, the idea that there are dreams in search of a dreamer has had currency. It may be that through the development of social dreaming, which sees the dream as belonging to the matrix and not the individual, we will be able to use dreams to inform our daily lives in a much more systematic fashion than hitherto. What has been discovered is that the experience of taking part in a social dreaming matrix leads to dreams being remembered increasingly and accessed through free association and amplification.

CHAPTER ONE

"Won from the void and formless infinite": experiences of social dreaming

W. Gordon Lawrence

The dream is a little hidden door in the innermost and most secret recesses of the soul opening into that cosmic night which was psyche long before there was any ego-consciousness and which will remain psyche no matter how far our ego-consciousness may extend. For all ego-consciousness is isolated: it separates and discriminates, knows only particulars and sees only what can be related to the ego. Its essence is limitation, though it reaches to the farthest nebulae among the stars. All consciousness separates but in dreams we put on the likeness of that more universal, truer, more eternal man dwelling in the darkness of primordial night. There he is still the whole and the whole is in him, indistinguishable from pure nature and bare of all egohood. It is from these all-uniting depths that the dream arises be it never so childish, grotesque, and immoral. So flower-like is it in its candour and veracity that it makes us blush for the deceitfulness of our lives.

Jung, 1953, p. 46

The Blind Architect Dream

*The dream was of being at a dinner party in the Paris apartment of
friends. During it a visitor arrived from the provinces. He had to get
to a new cathedral because he was involved in its construction, and I
seemed to be the only person who knew where it was. He was very
insistent that he should go by taxi as he had travelled a long distance
by train that day. I went down with him to the street where the taxi
was waiting and gave precise instructions to the driver. It was only
later in the dream when talking with the fellow guests that I realized
that the stranger was a blind architect. I remember thinking in the
dream, "Who would employ a blind architect?" A deaf composer is
possible. Beethoven proved that. But a blind architect?*

This dream occurred in Belgium in the autumn of 1990 at
the beginning of a conference that included social dreaming
as an activity. The next day I offered the dream to my
colleagues during what is called the "Social Dreaming Matrix".
Among the associations to the dream was the suggestion that I was
the blind architect of social dreaming in that I had found a space
for thinking about dreaming which no one had used before. What
was to be in that space was in the process of being discovered by
those who take part in this activity called social dreaming.

In outlining the development of social dreaming, the difference
between "discovery" and "invention" is worth clarifying. Invention connotes a completed innovation that is tangible or definable,
like a steam engine, or a concept such as "social class". An invention can only be improved through modification. Its essence
cannot be altered, or it is a new invention. Discovery is different in
that it leads to more and more disclosures and revelations as long
as there are people to experience and perceive.

My colleague David Armstrong offered a tighter distinction
given by Roger Penrose in his book *The Emperor's New Mind* (1989).
In it, Penrose discusses computers, minds, and the laws of physics
and asks if mathematics is an invention or a discovery. He argues
that mathematicians are really discovering truths that are independent of the mathematician's existence because they are already
"there". The examples he gives are of such structures as the
Mandelbrot set and complex numbers.

Penrose discriminates between discovery and invention by saying that discoveries

> . . . are the cases where much more comes out of the structure than is put into it in the first place. One may take the view that in such cases the mathematicians have stumbled upon "works of God". However there are other cases where the mathematical structure does not have such a compelling uniqueness, such as when, in the midst of a proof of some result, the mathematician finds the need to introduce some contrived and far from unique construction in order to achieve some very specific end. In such cases no more is likely to come out of the construction than was put into it in the first place and the word "invention" seems more appropriate than "discovery". These are indeed just "works of man". [pp. 96–97]

To illustrate succinctly: Freud did not invent "transference", he discovered it.

But how does a discovery generate revelations by others? Bion writes to the effect that if we are to get beyond "memory and desire"—the memory of past experiences and insights and the desire for particular kinds of experience—we have to experience a "blindness" because that is how we discover what is already there but has never been lodged here in our ken. Bion (1975), in the second of his Brazilian lectures, says that Freud, in correspondence with Lou Andreas-Salomé, wrote "that when he was investigating a very dark subject he sometimes found it illuminating to investigate it by *artificially blinding himself*" (italics added). Bion goes on to say that perhaps Milton's blindness was induced by the unconscious need to be so in order that he could investigate "those things invisible to man", which he reveals in Book III of *Paradise Lost*. This idea of artificially blinding oneself, which is a creative posture, is a key element of the capacity to be available for discovery (Bion, 1975, pp. 62–63). Such a posture is one that yields the kind of original and intense insights that are "Won from the void and formless infinite".

A gloss on this notion of blindness and creativity would be the deafness of Beethoven. While his deafness made him irascible and had a bad effect on his personal relationships, it had the opposite effect on his capacity to compose. Anthony Storr, in his book *The School of Genius*, quotes from a study of Beethoven.

In his deaf world, Beethoven could experiment with new forms of experience, free from the intrusive sounds of the external environment; free from the rigidities of the material world; free, like the dreamer to combine and recombine the stuff of reality, in accordance with his desires, into previously undreamed-of forms and structures. [Solomon, 1978, quoted in Storr, 1988, p. 52]

Social dreaming, it is being postulated, has been a discovery. To discover the dimensions of the conceptual space in which to locate social dreaming, it has been necessary, first, to blind oneself to conventional and received opinions about the ways to understand or interpret dreams, to experience dreams as phenomena in their own right, to rid oneself of *a priori* frameworks for limiting the nature of dreams. In this, I have not always been successful.

Second, the sense of experimenting with "new forms of experience" has been possible through David Armstrong, who read drafts of this chapter to make links and associations to the ideas that I was offering which generated further thoughts. We continued to discover the text and so to give voice to thoughts unspoken.

What I offer here is a description of a method of working with dreams which is in the making. As yet I do not fully understand what I am doing, but, as more and more colleagues join me, at times I get glimpses. And I am only at the stage of making notes, so to speak, towards a conceptualization, formulating "visions or dreams of conclusions", to borrow a phrase from Robert Jay Lifton (1987). What is written here is exploratory, and the reader may well discover more than I have.

Experiences towards a discovery

There is a particular form of education that uses the capacity to learn directly from experience both the conscious and the unconscious processes of being in group life. It stems from the work of Bion (1961) on experiences in groups. Like anyone who has been involved in understanding the unconscious life of institutions in this Bion tradition, I have had the experience of hearing a dream from a group participant which was clearly a dream that belonged to the group because it spoke in some way to the emergent life of it. With such dreams I had always been very cautious, not wanting to devalue them in any way by naive or wild interpretation. But always I felt inadequate to work with them, and any associations that I might have had I thought to be pedestrian. I called these "group" dreams and sometimes, in my mind, "social" dreams.

This was because I had learned, in some measure, to work with dreams in my own psychoanalysis, and so I was predisposed to see dreams as being a personal possession. Whatever the penumbral associations I might have, they were centred on myself and my past and present life and, as I recall, arose from the sense of deadness of any analysand. Probably like most other analysands, I can still remember the dream that I brought for my first session. Anything more I read on dreams confirmed in me the view that dreams were a gift from the unconscious to be interpreted in personal terms.

Nevertheless, like anyone who has read anthropological texts, I was fascinated by the way that so-called primitive peoples made use of their dreams. The people of the Kalahari desert, written about by Laurens Van der Post (1986), were able to use their dreams to illumine their daily lives and vice versa.

On a trip to Taiwan in 1985 I found through the Maryknoll missionaries that the aborigines of Taiwan told fortunes by means of dreams. In fact, the practice of oneiromancy was common for gauging the future or assessing misfortune in daily life. When tribes went hunting or head-hunting or had a particular religious service, the plan or start was made when the chief, the priest, or the initiator had a good dream. If a hunter had a bad dream after the hunt started, either he was sent home, or the party all rested until someone dreamt a good one. All the key events in life, such as marrying, opening up new land, building a house, were decided by means of oneiromancy. Illness, too, was treated by such means.

The Taiwan aboriginal tribes used their dreams so frequently that they had a taxonomy of good and evil dreams. For example, to dream of the sea was to predict that there would be good crops. To be cut by others or to fall into water was an evil dream. To dream of a freshly cut-off head on the eve of head-hunting was a good dream, as was the dream of having pleasure in sexual intercourse. To dream of having to clean the toilet meant that there would be no game on the next hunt (Ogawa & Asai, 1930).

There is a long history of using dreams in Western civilizations, but this use has tended to be viewed as being superstitious and unscientific. The books for interpreting dreams, of which there have been many over the centuries, were designed for those whose lives were dictated by fate, chance, and hardship. They are still available in various forms and tend to be dictionaries of dream symbolism.

An exception is the work of the Marquis de Saint-Denys, who published in 1867 *Les Rêves et les Moyens de les Diriger*, which resulted from his study of dreams from the age of 13. His interest was what was later to be called "lucid dreaming", which is the same as the techniques employed by the Tibetan Yogis. Rereading the book recently, I was struck by how ordinary he makes dreaming and how contemporary-sounding is his thinking as he writes about memory and dreams, the association of ideas, how to guide dreams, and transformations and transitions in dreams.

Among all these scattered pieces of information, there were two facts that I held in my mind: the dream that is offered in a group which is beyond the individual dreamer's personal life and which speaks to the life of the group, and the accounts of the use of dreams by primitive peoples. I vaguely felt that there had to be a connection between the two, but it was beyond me.

In addition, I had been very impressed by Jung's experience of having visions about political events, which he describes in the book *Memories, Dreams, Reflections* (1964). There he recounts that towards the summer of 1913 he felt himself to be in a state of pressure. The source of this pressure he perceived as existing in concrete reality and not coming psychically from himself. He goes on to say:

> In October while I was alone on a journey, I was suddenly seized by an overpowering vision: I saw a monstrous flood covering all the northern and low-lying lands between the North Sea and the Alps. When it came up to Switzerland I saw that the mountains grew higher and higher to protect our country. I realized that a frightful catastrophe was in progress.

I saw the mighty yellow waves, the floating rubble of civiliza-
tion, and the drowned bodies of uncounted thousands. Then
the whole sea turned to blood. The vision lasted about an
hour. I was perplexed and nauseated, and ashamed of my
weakness. [p. 169]

This vision recurred, leading Jung to conclude that he was
"menaced by psychosis". Because of this perception, if he was
asked by others about the political future of Europe he could only
reply that he did not have any thoughts on the matter.

In the spring and summer of 1914, he had three repetitions of
a dream in which *Europe was covered in ice as a result of Arctic cold.*
The cold, as he puts it, "descended from out of the cosmos". The end of the
dream was of everything flowering in the land, and there was a profusion
of grapes which he proceeded to distribute to a large crowd.

In July 1914 he was invited by the British Medical Association
to give a lecture in Aberdeen, "On the Importance of the Unconscious in Psychopathology". He says that as a result of this invita-
tion, important in itself, he was prepared for something fateful to
happen because it came when he was bombarded by such visions
and dreams. As a consequence, his life-work became defined.

On 1st August the world war broke out. Now my task was
clear: I had to understand what had happened and to what
extent my own experience coincided with mankind in general.
Therefore my first obligation was to probe the depths of my
own psyche. [Jung, 1964, p. 170]

If any justification is needed for listening to the messages of one's
visions and dreams, it is there in Jung's experiences.

By chance—or serendipity or providence or whatever—the
fourth fact presented itself. I read in a footnote in some book a
reference to *The Third Reich of Dreams* by Charlotte Beradt (1968).
Before obtaining the book, I felt intuitively that this was the link
for which I had been searching. Charlotte Beradt collected 300
dreams by Germans between 1933 and 1939, at which point she
had to leave Germany for America. Most of these she took down
from people herself, and this was supplemented by a doctor friend
who was able to query his patients unobtrusively. These dreams
she noted in code and hid in the spines of the books in her library.
Subsequently, she was able to send them to different addresses

abroad, where they were kept till she herself left Germany. It was some years later that she came to evaluate her material, when there was a large body of historical facts on the Nazi regime available through documents and research. During the war she published only one paper, called "Dreams under Dictatorship".

The events that lie behind the varied dreams she collected were explicit. They sprang "from man's paradoxical existence under a twentieth century totalitarian regime" (Beradt, 1968, p. 15)—that is, Hitler's Germany. Beradt makes the point that these dreams were not the products of unresolved inner personal conflicts either of the present or the past,

> . . . but arose from conflicts into which these people had been driven by a public realm in which half-truths, vague notions, and a combination of fact, rumour, and conjecture had produced a general feeling of uncertainty and unrest. These dreams may deal with disturbed human relations but it was the environment that had disturbed them. . . . [They] stemmed directly from the political atmosphere in which these people lived. . . . They are almost conscious dreams. Their background is clearly visible and what lies on their surface lies also at their roots. There is no facade to conceal associations, and no outside person need provide the link between dream image and reality—this the dreamer himself does. [pp. 14–15]

In the same book, Bruno Bettelheim writes an essay in which he argues that Beradt is too simplistic in her explanation. He postulates that the dreams "have their roots in the inner conflicts evoked by social realities within the person who dreams them". Be that as it may, Bettelheim concedes that under a system of terror people have to purge even their unconscious mind of any desire to fight back or of any belief that rebellion can succeed, because that is the only way that they can be safe. Any expression of hatred or of resistance endangers one's life. Therefore, Bettelheim argues, we cannot feel safe until we are certain that not even the unconscious can push us towards a dangerous thought or action. This is why Hitler was not assassinated. If the tyrant is not destroyed early enough, then his total control, once established, undermines the belief that any resistance can succeed (Beradt, 1968, p. 156).

Bettelheim assesses Beradt's work using an *a priori* framework that is exclusively psychoanalytic. The originality and sheer courage of what she did is acknowledged, but I find the tone of the discussion carping.

Having read Beradt's book, I was stunned by the potential of what she had achieved. What would happen if we had some Mass Observation-like study of dreams in the United Kingdom at different points in history? (Reading Benton's, 1990, biography of Naomi Mitchison, the Scottish writer, I find that she included her dreams in the accounts she wrote for Mass Observation.) For the moment, after reading Beradt, I was content to play with the idea of having a group of people who would dream socially, in the sense that I was using that adverb.

In what were to be my last months at the Tavistock Institute of Human Relations in 1982, I put on such a group with Patricia Daniel, a psychoanalyst who had long experience of working with groups in the Bion tradition. As we discussed the project beforehand, it was she who said that we ought to call it a "matrix" because this would allow us to suspend temporarily notions about group processes. At this point, we did not want this latter aspect to be part of the equation, so to speak, because we felt that the focus on the group process could take us away from the work of understanding the dreams. In other words, we were not interested in having a "dreaming group". Another way of looking at this is to say that we wanted to name a configuration that would carry out certain activities—the nature of which we were not certain. "Matrix", derived from the Latin for uterus, was chosen because it is a "place out of which something grows". We decided that the best arrangement of the chairs would be in the form of a spiral so that people could have their backs to others and be situated at different angles. A group would tend to arrange the chairs in the form of a circle.

The other procedures we established were that we could ask questions and make associations, and our work would be focused on that. We were both certain that the dream was not to be seen in any way therapeutically and that we were temporarily to rid our minds of clinical connotations. The matrix was to be an aid for cultural enquiry to be conducted through dreams. Because of our experience of taking groups in the Bion tradition, we puzzled a lot about the place of transference in the sense of what authority we would have to make our roles and what authority the participants might have to make this activity. The dream was to be the currency of the situation rather than the relationships between and among the participants and ourselves. What reality and significance all this would have, we were prepared to discover. We did not know what was right, so we fully expected to get things wrong.

We ran, then, for eight weeks a programme called a "Project in Social Dreaming and Creativity". It was composed of weekly ninety-minute sessions named as a "Social Dreaming Matrix". The sponsor was the Group Relations Training Programme of the Tavistock Institute, of which I was then joint director. The primary task (purpose) was "To associate to and interpret the potential social content and meanings of participants' dreams" (Lawrence, 1989).

What was clearly established in this first venture was that people could have dreams that had a social dimension. So the principal hypothesis was substantiated. At the end of this project, it could be said that:

> ... it [can] be hypothesized with more firmness that it is possible to have dreams which speak of our unconscious fears and anxieties about the society in which we live. The individual dreams around certain basic themes such as the family, work and relationships with parents, and similar significant others. Society however only exists "in the mind" as a construction of individuals based on their experiences of relationships with others with whom they happen to be connected. [Lawrence, 1989, p. 80]

In that same paper I went on to say something that I have now substantially revised: "By being able to disentangle the latent from the manifest content of social dreams there is a realizable possibility of identifying the unconscious relatedness of the individual to society" (p. 79).

Then there was a gap of six years. I went to the Shell International Petroleum Company for three years and afterwards was invited to join the International Foundation for Social Innovation in Paris as president.

But chance or serendipity or providence was at work . . .

The discovery of experiences

Through the Foundation in Paris, we held a working conference in Israel in 1987 on the theme of leadership and innovation. For 1988, I was asked by Vered Amitzi and Hanni Biran of Innovation and Change in Society (Israel) to provide some form of training for therapists and organizational consultants that would be experiential and germane to their *métiers*. As I thought about it, I decided that here was an opportunity to try the social dreaming matrix again and to build a programme around it, thinking that, to the best of my knowledge, there had been no attempt to link dreaming with professional practice except in terms of psychoanalytic training.

The details of this new programme of Dialogues—"Social Dreaming, Consultancy and Action-Research"—were that we started on a Sunday evening with an opening plenary. My idea was that people should be "on site" in order to dream before the first social dreaming matrix, which was at 8 a.m. on the Monday. The programme lasted till Thursday evening. Each day there were two matrices, first thing in the morning and last thing in the evening. All in all, there were seven of these. In-between there were what I called "Dialogues" and "Mutual Consultation Sets".

In designing the programme, I was concerned that there be opportunities for thinking about practice. Dialogues I regarded as one such opportunity and the consultation sets as another. The former were an opportunity to be available for thoughts. One staff member introduced a topic for ten to twenty minutes (no more than twenty), and the remainder of the session was used for mental associations and thinking further thoughts. Among the topics were "To Surprise the Soul" and "Psychoanalysis and Organizations". On this particular programme, I included a showing of the film *Who's in Charge?*, which Allan King and I had made for the Canadian Broadcasting Corporation. This is a film of working with a group of unemployed Canadians and was designed to enable them to find their authority to interpret their state.

The mutual consultation sets were opportunities for participants to examine their own case material in a disciplined manner using both systemic and psychoanalytic insights.

Why this kind of structure? I wanted to have the social dreaming matrices set in a context that was work- and reality-orientated. I did not want social dreaming to be some marginal activity. And clearly I wanted to see if there were links to be made between working in, say, a bank or an industrial enterprise as an organizational consultant and social dreaming.

The opening plenary for the whole programme was held on Sunday evening as the first working-day after Sabbath. Because the air-conditioning was very noisy I had switched it off, for otherwise I would not have been heard. My memory is of thirty-two people facing me, all anxious and all complaining of the heat. My colleagues had never taken such a programme before and were also anxious. I, at least, could imagine what it might be like. I introduced the programme by giving something of its history and then asked for people's feelings and associations to being present in it. One participant, whom I came to respect very much, was a distinguished professor with a Jungian background. She pointed out that there was nothing new in this programme because the Jungians had been doing it for years. I let her remark pass.

In the night that followed I had a vivid dream. *I was busy writing. Page after page flowed effortlessly from my fountain-pen. I would cast the pages aside on the floor, as I needed uncluttered space on my desk. What was I writing? The truth about Israel, no less! And I knew it was true. It had never been so clear for me. Then I realized that, as I wrote the last sentences on each page, the first ones on it were beginning to fade. The truth was as evanescent as a snowflake.*

Israeli dreams

All in all, there were about sixty to seventy dreams in the programme as a whole. The first dream that a participant presented was about mice. In reality, there were mice in the building because it was in the countryside, and I assumed they were field mice, though I never encountered any. Mixed-in was a remark that the way that we were sitting—with the chairs arranged in a spiral—was as though we were in layers.

At this moment my anxiety was overwhelming. Here was I in a roomful of Israelis, with the exception of three, having a series of associations that were frightening: mice—rats—the Nazi propaganda that Jews = rats = vermin = extermination = people in layers in mass graves. I kept silent, thinking to myself that it was for others to make the connections.

The sixth speaker—and here I am talking of a very short period of time—referred to a dream of *people dividing into couples, going in different directions. She said that there was a smell of old clothes.*

This fuelled my associations. But I kept silent, because I felt that to offer them would be an intrusion from an outsider who had a different racial history—who had been a spectator, so to speak, rather than a participant. As I always feel when working in Israel, I was in a roomful of people whose shared history and individual family tragedies are too much for any human being to support.

I now feel differently about that particular event. I should have had the courage to voice my associations, which were subliminal for the remainder of the programme. The one defence that I can offer is that I had yet to discover the containing capacity of the matrix. I knew this capacity intuitively but obviously not enough to have faith in it and in the participants who were creating it.

This burden of tragedy was illustrated in part by one participant who said that he had come to the programme because he could not dream. He was an immigrant from Russia. Imagine my joy to see him in one session with a little notebook in which he had written down his dream. It was of *Israel as a great, smooth slab of marble in which there were no cracks, no place, no dirt, no soil, for anything to grow.*

I had felt that transference would play little part in a social dreaming matrix—or rather I could not see how it could be used for the "work" of the matrix, unlike a conventional group where transference is of the essence of its life.

I was wrong. On the morning of the third day, one of the oldest-looking men in the room, with the silver hair of cliché, opened the matrix. He said that he never remembered the past, that he made a point of getting on with life in the here-and-now, but last night he had had three dreams. The first saw him *as a young naval officer caught in a storm.* The second was of *running refugees from boats into Israel, near Haifa, after the war, at the time of the British Mandate*. The third was of *taking such refugees by truck into the desert and of giving them supplies and tools and having to say: this is where you will live.*

I cannot convey how moving these accounts were. He was near to tears, and the room was at one with him as he spoke. For myself, I knew that I had to keep my eyes fixed on him so that whenever he looked at me he would be supported in some way.

The associations were to the Mandate and to the history of Israel. The fact that I, the sole native Britisher, was present was, I am hypothesizing, a link between the matrix and the dreams. I base this on the absence of historical facts in the matrix.

In the matrix, because of the external noise and English being spoken with pronounced accents, I sometimes misheard. There was a good deal of talk of what I thought was the "empty father". Was it the matrix, the consultants? No, I was wrong, what they were talking of was *intifada*. This raised questions for the participants about their own history of persecution and the despairing feelings they had about *intifada*. They were quick to point out that identification with the aggressor is a real phenomenon.

I take a sequence of dreams from one dreamer at random and quote from the notes (trying as well as I can to reproduce the fragmentary nature of the account). *He has a central feeling of weakness, of inability to have control over the situation.* [In reality, he had had a telephone call to collect his daughter from the airport and found that he had lost his identity card, which is very symbolic]. *He felt that he wanted to be here and there at the same time—a split. The plane was late. . . . He is in an ocean, he fights the waves, he wants to survive. . . . He comes to an office in the kibbutz and he finds there are people who are already there and he doesn't feel easy with the situation. . . . He tries different things that don't go together in the kibbutz. He wants to find a solution to the problem of private and collective things going together—a wedding for example. He has the feeling that each time he awakes, the solution he already found in his dream has got lost.*

David Armstrong, on reading this passage on the Israeli dreams, offered me a number of associations. His view is that much of the content is about the matrix itself, or rather the experience of it. Will anything grow in this "marble" of a matrix? Who is the "empty father", the empty consultant–founder?

There was surprise, at times, that dreams were fragmentary, as if the wish were to have "whole" dreams whose manifest content could be quickly translated in terms of the latent content. At the beginning, I had said to my colleagues that we should just try to work with the fragments and that we should not succumb to the desire to provide all-embracing interpretations—act out some "saviour" role for Israel as though we were members of the Diaspora come home to put things right.

At the end of the Israel programme, I was well enough pleased. We had established, once again, that people can dream socially if invited to do so. The idea that the matrix exists in its own right but is also a refractor of phenomena from the societal context seemed to have more substance. I toyed with the idea of the matrix as a prism. The dialogues had been stimulating, and the mutual consultation sets had given participants opportunities to reflect systemically on their roles in their outside organizations.

The particular situation of Israel as a state and its unique political position in the Middle East had been present in the dreams in a way that was quite profound. People who took part said that the experience of the activity of dreaming socially and the ability to make associations allowed them to reflect on their professional roles in a richer way than they had hitherto experienced. Most important of all, we had seen that dreams are part of the stuff of living and not some specialized activity.

Because of the enthusiasm of international colleagues, there followed a series of such programmes in Germany (1989), Sweden (1989), the United Kingdom (1989, 1990), Australia (1989), and America (1990). All were basically of the same design as the original in Israel. In most of these programmes, there were about sixty to eighty dreams presented.

German dreams

In Germany, it was agreed that dreams be given in German and English; in the main, people were able to translate for themselves. While it slowed down the pace, I felt that this gave us more time to reflect. Translation is usually felt to be constricting; however, at the end of the programme most people remarked that translation could be a transformation—that is, in giving the dream in another language, new aspects of meaning could be found—and could thereby be enriching. This point about translation, I see with hindsight, is consistent with the social processes of "opening out" through association and elaboration which seem to be engendered by the social dreaming matrix.

As the dreams had unfolded from the participants, I had been struck, given the ages of the majority, that there was no explicit reference to the war. I was, of course, carrying the memory of the Israel programme and aware of the pioneering work of Charlotte Beradt. One participant, who worked as an expert in politics and economics in a South American country, would make references to his feeling of dread about being in a fascist regime there. He had a lot of dreams on that theme. South America, I felt, was some kind of displacement.

I was in a dilemma. I felt that if I, working as a matrix-taker, so to speak, was to introduce the theme of Nazism and the war, I would be bringing in a political element for which there was no clear evidence except for the "fascist" dreams but which I felt had to be in the unconscious. I spoke about this to my two consultant colleagues, explaining my difficulty, saying that I could not understand that such a formative experience for so many in the programme was being avoided, denied, or just plain forgotten.

How the evidence came to the surface was striking. The sole exclusively German-speaking participant gave a dream the day after this discussion with my colleagues. *He was in a cemetery and in it there were three bushes [drei Buchen]. There were no people.* After discussion among the participants, this phrase *drei Buchen* was translated as "three beeches", and we thought little of it as we each puzzled on what the dream might mean. It was only in the consultants' discussion afterwards that my German colleague Burkard Sievers suddenly exclaimed, "There it is, *drei Buchen—Buchen—Buchenwald!*" In a real sense, it was a relief for us. While two of us have known each other for about twenty years, and the third member is near my age, we had never spoken about the war years and our experiences. But we did that evening.

We shared this in a subsequent plenary discussion with the participants. One man told of a recurrent dream since childhood during the war but never reported in the matrix; others spoke of what they had had to do to suppress their memories.

Something of the extraordinariness of dreaming comes out. Again, I take one at random from my notes. A woman dreamt that *enemies stole a baby, who could be her son. A woman appeared who had a saucepan for a nose and a trombone for an ear. A man and wild animals pursued her. She had the miraculous ability to fly, but she lost this ability. Just then a parabolic disc fell from the sky. There was smoke and gas. She tried to save herself and the baby. There was a great smell. She escaped, but there was an explosion.* The images of the dream as it unfolded became more and more Hieronymus Bosch-like in my mind. The associations were about the Apocalypse.

With hindsight, could this dream, in 1989, have been anticipating a united Germany and the fantasies that a lot of people held about a possible repetition of the war years if Germany were to be reunited?

Australian dreams

Speaker: *"I'm in the dissecting room of the University of Padua. The cadaver is a woman."*

"Is that it?" someone asked.

"It's the fifteenth century." He then went on to say that at that time there were two ways of conceptualizing the human body, because of opposing scientific orientations. In some ways, this was a mirroring of the programme, which was using and looking at dreams in a way that was different from the conventional psycho-analytic one.

There was at times in the programme an idealization of the Aborigine as a dreamer. We felt that we were lacking a critical element of Australian life by not having an Aborigine among us. This led to explorations of political life in Australia, with its short roots in the cultures of the Northern Hemisphere, which denies the tremendously long history of the Aborigines.

One woman participant had a vivid dream of identification with an Aboriginal woman. For the time she was recounting it, one felt what it might be like to be in the skin of such a woman suffering the degradations of contemporary Australian urban life.

A dream that was repeated was of balloons. The first was of *a huge inflated condom in the sky which was like a Zeppelin*. The programme ended with an association to a French film (*The Red Balloon*) in which a small boy, in order to save his balloon from being punctured by bullies, lets it slip from his fingers and float upwards to the sky. While I felt that there was a need to have a uniting symbol to end the work of the matrix, I could accept that the balloon was representative of dreaming which is not to be punctured because it is freeing in its own right.

Because we were in the land of dreams with its dream paintings, I visited the National Gallery of Victoria in Melbourne to view Aboriginal art, which derives from the Australian Aboriginal myths of creation. There are variations from tribe to tribe, but essentially the myths are the same. The common element would be that, in what is called the "Dreamtime", in the long-distant past the earth was flat and featureless. The earth then was peopled with giant, semi-human beings who were like animals but also behaved like men and women. They came out of the earth, where they had slumbered for countless time. These Dreamtime heroes did all the things that Aborigines do today. But the Dreamtime came to an end, and, where these creators had been active, the land took its shape: an isolated hill, a watercourse, or some other natural feature came into existence. The Dreamtime heroes shaped the land and shaped the daily lives of present Aborigines and even formulated the laws that determine all aspects of secular and sacred life today.

The similarities between the myths of Australian Aborigines and those other cultures nearer to home are easy to find—the gods of Olympia, who shaped the mountains and the volcanoes, peopled ancient Greece; the sagas of the Nordic races describe how the gods made the complete universe. So dream and myth are inexorably linked, and it seems to be accepted that life as it is lived now was once embedded in dream (Roberts & Mountford, 1965, pp. 9–15).

Before me I have a reproduction of *Ipalu: Bush Banana Painting*. What strikes me is the almost Mandelbrot-set–like qualities of the patterns in the painting. These patterns have morphological meaning, with their roundels and paths. Peter Sutton, in *Dreamings: The Art of Aboriginal Australia* (1988), analyses this morphology. In very crude ways, the fashion in which dreams and associations are linked in the life of a matrix could be represented morphologically.

* * *

The experiences from the social dreaming matrices held in Sweden, America, and Britain further demonstrated that people very quickly learn to dream socially and to have associations to their dreams. What is also apparent is the wonder of the possession of an unconscious and the ability of human beings to romp in the theatres of their minds.

Some experiences of the experience

As the concept of the social dreaming matrix has evolved, there have been more and more discoveries, and these are very much in the Elizabethan sense of the word "revealing".

The "ideology of the individual dream"

Alastair Bain, originator of the Australian Institute of Social Analysis, wrote to me in a letter that "there is a real struggle in letting go of the ideology of the individual dream and the associated notion of possessiveness".

Our contemporary thinking about dreams derives from Freud, who caused us to take dreams seriously. Any exploration of dreaming has to start from his work and from that of the great psychologists, like Jung, who followed. Freud was a clinician, so it was the individual who was his focus. He held a "neurophysiological, energetic model of the mind", and, in the words of Meltzer (1984), he had a tendency to treat "hypotheses as if they were observed facts" (p. 23).

Irrespective of his orientation, Freud developed a number of concepts that are with us today. He made the formulations that the dream was the "guardian of sleep" and elaborated on "the dream as wish-fulfilment". "Manifest and latent content" was a key conceptualization, as was the "dream censor" and also "dream-work". These have been the essential tools in conventional dream analysis. In his far-reaching analysis, Meltzer (1984) argues that there is no evidence that the dream is either the guardian or the destroyer of sleep. He also questions what Freud meant by "wish", and he writes that "a wish is something that envisages its fulfilment without consideration of the means required for its fulfilment" (p. 12).

Erich Fromm (1980) has also questioned Freud's position on wishes:

> Instead of assuming that the dream is the distorted presentation of a wish, one may formulate the hypothesis that the dream represents any feeling, wish, or thought that is sufficiently important to be present during our sleep, and that its appearance in dreams is a sign of its importance. In my observation of dreams, I have found that many dreams do not contain a wish but offer insight into one's own situation or into the personality of others. [p. 72]

Currently, much of what Freud proposed on dreams is being re-evaluated by a new generation of psychoanalysts.

The ideology of the individual dream in the context of psychoanalysis makes sense. It is a logical consequence. The dreamer and the analyst are in a dyadic exploration in which transference feelings are a critical dimension. Any significant other persons are held in mind by the two subjectively. The focus is on the inner world of the individual situated in the environment.

I have, however, a nagging concern that the popular excitement about the individual dream is because it feeds narcissistic preoccupations. In the West, we live in cultures that have such qualities. The individual comes to feel no interest in the future and regards history as an encumbrance (Lasch, 1979). There is an irrational belief that the individual is a self-contained system, complete in him- or herself. The dream, if regarded only as a personal possession, can, at worst, reinforce this separation from the world.

This way of construing dreams is understandable because not only has dreaming become important in the therapeutic world—itself an invention of this century—but also the twentieth century has seen the triumph of the "I". We are preoccupied with ego-consciousness. Our feelings, our wishes, motivations, and will are mediated by the "I" in relation to the outer world in which we live. There is a tendency to regard the "I-ness" as being pre-eminent.

But late in this century we are beginning to struggle to redis-cover our connectedness to the environment in which we live. Among the positive benefits of the Green Revolution and ecologi-cal awareness is the emergent re-conceptualization of the nature of the relatedness between the individual and the cosmos. That we live in an ecosystem is now difficult to deny.

This ideology of individualism has been expressed by and through poets since the seventeenth century. John Holloway (1977) argues that poets have been expressing their wish to find the terms of life for themselves by undergoing some spiritual journey on their own to find insight. While this has led to new forms and genres in English poetry, it has smacked of arrogance, even steril-ity, as individuals have attempted to seek out fundamental truths for themselves in their own terms.

Something of this is reflected in the enormous growth in the "human relations" industry of counselling, therapy, and interven-tions like assertiveness training. At their worst, all reinforce the personal boundaries around the individual and the "I", separating people, making them believe that they are unique and differentiat-ing them from others and the events and phenomena in their worlds. The concern for others inevitably diminishes as the indi-vidual thrusts to a position of—sometimes ruthless—self-fulfil-ment or self-actualization. The dream can be used as grist for this mill of self-aggrandizement.

On the other hand, the social dreaming matrix, it can be postu-lated, asks for dreams that go beyond the individual and are focused on the environment. During the day, as individuals we emphasize our autonomy and the nature of the boundaries that separate us from other people and make us unique. But our dreams are organized on a different basis. As Ullman (1981) puts it:

> Our dreams are more concerned with the nature of our con-nections with all others. The history of the human race, while awake, is a history of fragmentation, of separating people and communities of people nationally, religiously, politically. Our dreams are connected with the basic truth that we are all

members of a single species. While awake we move through our lives in a sequential, linear moment-by-moment fashion with a point representing birth and another point the present moment. But when we go to sleep and begin to dream we create pictures of what's going on in our psyche from points of space and time which are outside of our waking organizations. [p. 1]

It seems to me now that this inherent quality of the dream—to be connected—is the one on which to concentrate in order to be able to discover meaning in these social, even cosmic, terms.

The primary task

Since I started this activity of social dreaming, there has been a substantial shift in my thinking about the primary task, as I indicated earlier. What Meltzer (1984) has to say about manifest and latent content is highly pertinent. The point is that by postulating these two dimensions, Freud implied that the dreamer is tricky and must be hiding some information. It also leads to the idea that the dream is a puzzle to be solved like a "whodunit".

In the beginning of social dreaming, I tended to hold this viewpoint without questioning it and, indeed, had it in the primary task. Now I feel that the dream, the dreamer, and dreaming have to be celebrated and all valued in their own right. This merely reflects the thinking of Jung, who saw the dream in phenomenological terms and insisted that each dream is taken in its own right and its symbolism unravelled and decoded. In the dream, it is the "cryptic or hidden meaning", to use Meltzer's phrase, that one is discovering without assuming that there is an obscurity of meaning. This, Meltzer argues, was the logical error that trapped Freud, because of his preoccupation with showing that dreams were not nonsense and were to be taken very seriously. Freud overstated his case.

The primary task is now clearer for me because of the experience of working with it. The work is associative, not interpretative in the classical, clinical psychoanalytic sense. I now recast the primary task as: "To discover the social meanings of available dreams in the matrix."

This means that a lot of the work is left to the individual, who uses his or her authority to find meaning. At the present time, I am content to leave it all at the level of associations and meanings, identifying allegory and symbolism. I am anxious not to go beyond the evidence and am content to provide the resources and conditions for people to learn how to dream socially.

The matrix

The working hypothesis that I offer is that a social dreaming matrix exists to discover what only a social dreaming matrix can discover. That is its sole *raison d'être*.

To take the same thought processes as are used in psychoanalysis into a social dreaming matrix is not valid because, it is my hypothesis, a different version or even type of dream is evoked. More particularly, if the container system for receiving the dream is changed, the dream-contained will change.

For example, dreams can be interpreted in terms of the journeys of a hero. Jean and Wallace Clift, in their book *The Hero Journey in Dreams* (1988), have developed a beautifully coherent scheme for understanding the stories that people live by. The monomyth that we live by, they argue, using Jungian notions, can be divided into three phases: the Departure, the Initiation, and the Return. The hero-journey seminars that they organize make use of Ira Progoff's (1975) system of Intensive Journal Workshops, and within these seminars there are opportunities for dreaming. The dreams that the Clifts describe in their book can all be interpreted in terms of the hero journey. Here, I would hypothesize that it is the nature of the seminar-as-container that generates the dreams of the journeying of heroes.

The idea of the matrix has been central. Whereas in a group we search for a universe of meanings, in the matrix a multi-verse of meanings can coexist. If you think about it, once a dream is offered there can be as many associations as there are people in the room—and that's a lot of associations.

The way that the seats are arranged in the matrix tries to further the unique work of the participants in the matrix. Originally, seats were arranged in a spiral so that people were at different angles to one another. Now the design is a bit like a snowflake. The chairs are arranged in blocks of four in a diamond shape and linked to each other. All face in towards the centre.

In the American programme, the matrix was seen as an expanding universe with "black holes" of ignorance, not knowing, unknowing; perhaps as a representation of the cosmos. For myself, I think of the individuals in the matrix each with their personal world of other individuals alive and dead, so that the matrix is full of the shades of biographies (the dead are alive).

Bion (1975) wonders about the psychoanalytic theories of the mind, which sound like the astronomical theory of black holes, and asks which causes which. "Is this some peculiarity of the human mind which projects it up into space, or is this something real in space from which derives the idea of space in the mind itself?" (p. 104). He does see cosmology as a model for psychoanalysis but would use the latter as his starting point for investigating the human mind. With the matrix, do we have a representation of both the cosmos and the human mind to process dreams for their meanings?

For this kind of work, I am convinced that the matrix is a medium that gives a different message to participants than would a group. This is also expressed through the seating arrangements. There is not the tyranny of belonging to the group as a person—because it is the dream that is the medium for discourse, not the individual. One can feel disconnected, at times, in the matrix, but a connection can always be found because of the richness of the associative culture that it engenders.

What Freud wrote about the dream censor is of little value to us now, but the idea of "censorship" in a broader, literal sense is worth retaining. It is important in the social dreaming matrix that there be a work climate that is non-judgmental so that the people do not censor by laughing or disapproving. For example, a member of one matrix had a dream of *himself and his wife doing the washing together* [which they do in reality]; *they were sorting out underpants.* He and his wife buy the same pants and have done for years. Someone in the matrix grinned, so it was difficult for him to continue and he spoke of his embarrassment. He then went on to say that there was "a helluva difference when we put them on". Later in the conference he offered more dreams, one of which was *being at a circus of performing spiders; one spider could prance around the ring like a circus horse and even had a flowing mane.*

I think what excites me about the social dreaming matrix and the other events, particularly the dialogues, is that one does think new thoughts, and sometimes I am amazed to hear colleagues speak out thoughts that have been private for years or never thought before. The authority for this rests not on individuals but in the events and the work that they pursue.

More and more I begin to accept Bion's notion that we have to be available for thought—the notion that there are thoughts in search of a thinker. Can we extend this to think in terms of dreams in search of a dreamer? What I think the social dreaming matrix questions is the ideology that dreams belong to a person and are to be interpreted as such. This is not to devalue that kind of work—so important for myself in my own psychoanalysis. All I am saying is that the matrix produces different kinds of dreams through dreamers. The context is different, that is all.

The change of context changes the nature of the relationships among the participants. Earlier I said that I had been confused about the place of transference in the matrix and gave the example of the Israeli dreamer who spoke of the experiences of the past reworked through his dreams. I can now say that if the transference issues between the participants and the "takers" of it were to be addressed directly, it would rob the dreams of the opportunity to experience these issues of authority. The transference, if you will, has to become apparent in the dream; it is avoided if it is worked with directly in the here-and-now.

Recently a woman recounted her dream in a matrix that was being taken by another man and myself. Her dream was that *she had to go to her cousin's house to see his wife to say that she could not come to a party that was planned. She could not do so because she had to look after a child in connection with her work. As she stood in the hallway of the house of her cousin she noted that it was very narrow, and the stairs which went up to another floor took up most of the space. . . . The cousin's wife said "Isn't it horrible for that child?" and went on to recount very confidential information about the child. The dreamer had not said which child she was seeing and, anyway, the matter was very confidential. The dreamer had to listen to the cousin's wife and had to pretend that she did not know the details. The story was that the child had been conceived and borne by a woman who had a contract with a man to do so. The man wants the child because he and his male partner want to bring up a child.*

The dream can be seen as an attempt to work out the relatedness of the participants to the two male "takers" of this matrix: woman contracting = participant giving birth; child = dream; cousin's wife = the house in which the programme was being held, which was sponsored by another institution related to the dreamer's one.

* * *

Independently of me, David Armstrong has come to the same conclusion based on his re-reading of the dreams of the conferences that have been held in England.

The dream and the transcendent

When I see reproductions of Peter Bruegel the Elder's picture of the Tower of Babel, I am reminded of the matrix. The source for the biblical story of the Tower of Babel was the ziggurats built by the Ancient Babylonians. These towers symbolized the connection between humankind and the gods. While I am not suggesting that the matrix has the same qualities, I am intrigued by the notion that the dream offered in the matrix-as-ziggurat can link the individual dreamer with others and with all that is beyond, or transcendent, to them. There can, as well, be different "languages" through the associations, but people still communicate.

On the same theme, there is the classical dream of Jacob's Ladder, which Laurens Van der Post (1986) regards as "perhaps the greatest dream that has ever been dreamed in the history of man because it is a dream which conveys both its own message and at the same time tells us what dreaming is" (p. 79). This dream shows Jacob that there is reciprocity between man on earth and the forces of creation. The dream is a ladder up and down which messengers (Angels) move, influencing both God and man. There can be communication between the God in the mind and man on earth. Man is not just a thing to be ordered about but an imaginative, sentient being who can use his energies for creation.

Social dreaming offers us a way of conceptualizing human beings as being more complex than the behavioural psychologists
would have us believe. Dreams are not just neurons that are mis-
firing. Early anthropologists all put forward the idea that primitive
peoples believed that dreaming was the experience of the wandering soul during sleep. A. R. Radcliffe-Brown (1922), for example,
when describing the belief of the Andaman Islanders, writes:

> Dreams are sometimes explained by saying the dreamer's
> double (*ot-jumulo*) has left his body and is wandering else-
> where. Dreams are regarded as being veridical ... and a
> sleeper is not awakened lest his *ot-jumulo* or double be away
> from his body. [p. 166]

If we regard dreams as complex products of unconscious trains
of thought, day residues, wishes, and desires and recognize that
they are also shaped by the cultural beliefs of the society of which
the dreamer is a member, it can be hypothesized that the dream is
an intimation of a mental process that enables human beings to
give meaning to their waking life. Associating to the dream and
discovering its multifaceted meanings is a process of "deepening
events into experience ... through reflective speculation"
(Bleakley, 1989, p. 10). This is the work of the soul.

The dream can take us out of our body and untrammel us, at
the very least, from the nets of our conscious, logico-positivist
thinking. In a review of the available literature on the subject,
George Gillespie (1988) asks: "When does lucid dreaming become
transpersonal experience?" He concludes that there is no objective
way of establishing the truth or falsehood of the question, but his
conclusion deserves quotation:

> In the end, then, since we have no means to be certain that
> any apparent experience of God, *Brahman*, the void, *nirvana*,
> another plane of existence, or of any reality beyond the
> dreamer really is what it seems to be, a transpersonal experi-
> ence of transcendent reality begins when I believe it begins.

The observations, then, of the early anthropologists appear to
have validity in the sense that by the act of finding meaning to the
dream the soul is involved. Also the dream, by its nature, ushers us
into the presence of the transpersonal and transcendent, provided

that we have not cluttered the space for experiencing the event of the dream with our *a priori* notions and prejudices.

The dream ushers us into the numinous, but that could never be proven objectively.

The dream and everyday activities

As we have seen, the evidence that people directly linked dreams in the past to their everyday activities is not too difficult to find. Indians on the British Columbia frontier, for example, once possessed the power to use dreams for hunting:

> Some old-timers, men who became famous for their powers and skills, had been great dreamers. Hunters and dreamers. They did not hunt as people now do. They did not seek uncertainly for the trails of animals whose movements we can only guess at. No, they located their prey in dreams, found their trails, and made dream-kills. Then the next day, or a few days later, whenever it seemed auspicious to do so, they could go out, find the trail, re-encounter the animal, and collect the kill. . . .
>
> Today it is hard to find men who can dream in this way. There are too many problems. Too much drinking. Too little respect. People are not good enough now. Maybe there will again be strong dreamers when these problems are overcome. Then more maps will be made. New maps. [Brody, 1986, pp. 44–45]

An Israeli colleague, Michael Tiplitz, has offered an example of how this near-veridical ability can be mobilized. The decision before the secretariat of a kibbutz was about the kind of cash crop that they were to grow. The majority favoured cotton, which was a familiar adaptation. There was also an argument for alfalfa. The night before the decision was to be made, the general secretary dreamt of *being in a Chinese village surrounded by paddy fields for rice-growing. In the dream he felt peace.*

Tiplitz, who had been a participant at the first social dreaming programme in Israel, was working as a consultant with this secretariat. As he said, when he first reported this experience to me a year afterwards, "I'd learned to take dreams seriously, so when the secretary reported it I asked for associations and tried to work with it, which is something I'd never done in my consultancy before." The result was the decision that alfalfa would be the better crop. The secretary felt that his dream had clarified his own ambivalence.

Kilton Stewart (1969) provides a well-documented account of how dreams and everyday activities are linked to enhance the quality of living. In 1935, he was travelling through the unexplored rain forest of the Central Range of the Malay Peninsula. There he was introduced to the Senoi, whom he was to study for fifteen years. The Senoi, a jungle tribe, lived without conflict with neighbouring tribes, and they themselves had had no violent crimes for between two to three hundred years. He found that these qualities of social cooperation and integration were grounded in their system of psychology.

This system of psychology had two aspects: they were committed, first, to dream interpretation and, second, to dream expression, which took place in an "agreement trance" or cooperative reverie. Dream interpretation was a regular feature of their daily lives. A family would spend breakfast listening to each others' dreams and associating to them; afterwards, the head of the household would go to a council meeting to report, discuss, and analyse the dreams of the older children and the men in the community. What happened to women's dreams is not recounted.

Stewart describes the psychology of the Senoi thus:

... man creates features or images of the outside world in his own mind as part of the adaptive process. Some of these features are in conflict with him and with each other. Once internalized, these hostile images turn man against himself and against his fellows. In dreams man has the power to see these facts of his psyche, which have been disguised in external forms, associated with his own fearful emotions, and turn against him and the internal images of other people. [p. 161]

The Senoi believe that if the individual continues to think in this way and does not have the aid of his fellows in disentangling his feelings, he will end up by believing these hostile images and become psychologically and socially abnormal. Through being able to surface and analyse dreams, each individual can be master

of his own dream or spiritual universe by calling on the cooperation of the forces embedded there.

As children recount their dreams to an elder, they are transformed in their meaning. The child's common anxiety-dream of
falling, for instance, is responded to by the adult saying that it is a
wonderful dream and asking what was discovered on falling. If
the child says that he or she awoke before falling, it is pointed out
that every dream has a purpose and that the child should relax in
the dream because it is the quickest way to get in touch with the
powers of the spirit world. In time, this falling dream is changed
for the child from an anxiety-making one into the excitement of the
joy of flying.

Through these methods the child is initiated into a way of
thinking that will be developed for the rest of his or her life. As a
consequence, the members of the Senoi tribe discover their deepest
selves and are able to harness their creative powers.

Having made a comparative study of the dreams of the Senoi
tribe with the dreams of other cultures, Stewart concludes that:

> ... dreaming can and does become the deepest type of crea-
> tive thought. Observing the lives of the Senoi it occurred to me
> that modern civilization may be sick because people have
> sloughed off, or failed to develop, half their power to think.
> Perhaps the most important half. . . .
>
> In the West, the thinking we do while asleep usually re-
> mains on a muddled, childish, or psychotic level because we
> do not respond to dreams as socially important and include
> dreaming in the educative process. This social neglect of the
> side of man's reflective thinking, when the creative process is
> most free, seems poor education. [pp. 166–167]

In this century it has been the specialized discipline of psychoanalysis which has shaped our approach to understanding dreams,
and in the process we have lost the accumulated wisdom of so-
called primitive peoples to use dreams as part of our everyday life.
It can be argued that the activity of dreaming is redundant in a
specialized, highly technological world which is increasingly governed by the operations of information technology, but, as has been
hinted at in this chapter, people are increasingly aware that they
live in an ecosystem in which there are linkages that have been

unimagined hitherto, that they exist in a "wholeness" that can be but dimly perceived because of their own experiences of fragmentation. The critical relationship for human beings is between the conscious and unconscious dimensions of the mind. The artificial separation of these—or, more accurately, the inability to transact between the two with a Jacob's Ladder—furthers the fatal split between rationality and irrationality, thinking and feeling, good and evil, the sacred and the profane.

Thoughts for the future of social dreaming

Robert Jay Lifton (1987) writes:

> The dream, then, is central to our evolutionary heritage. In it we find, most profoundly, both clue to and expression of the human capacity for good and evil—for holding visions, for prospective imagination. More than ever, we must dream well if we are to further the wonderful, dangerous, and always visionary human adventure. [p. 194]

My interest is only with dreams that occur during sleep and my preoccupation is only with trying to disentangle their meanings through discovery in order to reveal any links between the unconscious and everyday life conducted in complex societies. The images that we have in our dreams are social in origin, but they become transformed, especially in psychoanalysis, in order to be used personally. This use of dreams I would want to preserve, but at the same time I am also interested in the added transformation of the personal into the social. The images are two-way in that they have something to say not only about unresolved challenges facing the individual, but also about the society in which the individual is located and conducts a life. The challenge of the moral issues engendered by *intifada*, for example, is both personal and social. It is the sons and daughters of both Israeli and Palestinian parents who have to go and fight. The excruciating agony and grief are personal. Dreams also point us to the limiting aspects of society, and when meaning is found to them they take us out of ourselves and enable us to be situated outside our skins (Ullman, 1989, p. 294). In this way, personal concern becomes transformed into social concern. The ruthlessness of the individual for narcissistic survival can be transformed into a ruth for the future of the species in a systemically linked cosmos.

So far it has been established that individuals can cooperate to dream socially. That these dreams, on occasion, can illuminate both the social and the political condition of a society has also been established. We expect a dream to be cryptic—after all, it comes from the unconscious. The discovery of social meanings is never easy. What may be more important than the "product" of the dream, the meanings, which can never be absolute, is the "process" of arriving at the range of meanings possible. It is this act of creativity that is the hallmark of social dreaming. This process could be a paradigm for discovering meaning for other linkages between phenomena and events in our environment. It is a process that encourages the reflective nature of human beings as they try to make sense of their experiences in both their social and their inner worlds.

As yet, there is no evidence that dreaming has been brought to the stage of development that was achieved by the British Columbian Indians or the Senoi tribe in Malaya. Perhaps, in time, this will be possible.

How social dreaming can illuminate the political milieu was illustrated in a programme of dialogues in Germany. My colleague Dieter Seiler and I were puzzled about why participants had more than usual difficulties in recalling their dreams. We talked of it and had the working hypothesis that, because of the reunification of Germany, there was an anxiety about remembering dreams because the last "dream" had been so horrendous. When we floated this hypothesis to the participants they, very movingly, told of what it was like to be in Germany now. They could never trust the kind of "dream" that had been before their parents. Significantly, there had been a lot of confusion as to what a "dream" was at the beginning of the programme. Was it a "vision", an imaginative act, a "daydream"? We had said that we were interested only in dreams that occurred during sleep.

Our hypothesis was confirmed. Now that Germany has been reunited, the people in the outside world in other countries have unspoken fantasies about what might happen in the future. At the same time, the Germans are fully aware that they are reluctant to have an identity. The last, now thankfully lost, identity was too much to bear.

Finally, I see social dreaming as being concerned with "revelation"—not in the apocalyptic sense, but in that of discovering meaning for being human at this point in history, for re-making the imago of this generation's relatedness between mankind and the cosmos as a way of continuing to re-conceptualize the relationships between human beings themselves and all that exists on the earth.

The spiritual search of social dreaming is fulfilled through relating the inside and outside realities of the individual. It is the dream, however, that links the individual to ultimate reality, which Bion signified as "O" (Bion, 1970). For a praying person, O will signify the godhead the person is experiencing; for a psychoanalyst, O is the upcoming emotional truth of a session. The dream, too, will have a real emotional truth. It is the work of discovering the meanings of the dream that can be seen as "trueing". Participating in a social dreaming matrix is an act of faith in the sense that there is faith in the possibility of having a dream that speaks out the truth if we can discern it. At the same time, we know that the truth can never be known. It is the unknowable that is the focus of our attention. This is the paradox. Trueing the dream may become, as it was in the past, a way to trueing our waking, quotidian lives as a continuous process of revelation.

CHAPTER TWO

Dreaming to learn:
pathways to rediscovery

Herbert Hahn

I n learning and teaching tasks, the unconscious processes at
work are often ignored. This contrasts to the analytic perspective where the evidence for underlying dynamics is sought
and their elucidation is given a central place. As workers in the
group-analytic field, we are often reminded that each individual
and group has to discover and rediscover unconscious processes
and that dreams are richly relevant. This chapter describes the
way in which specific discoveries of underlying dynamics in
groups and systems-as-a-whole occurred. It considers the worker's
vulnerability to becoming a collusive cog in an anti-development
wheel and focuses on the happy surprises that emerged when a
learning group shared their dreaming.

Dreams

With regard to working with dreams, my experience was that they
had a central place in psychoanalytic therapeutic work, and could
also be useful at times as grist to the mill in an educational context.

In a leaflet advertising one of the social dreaming programmes, the link between social dreaming and the management of transformations is made:

> In the past the "management of transformations" has been driven by the "politics of salvation". The process of consultancy and action-research to engender transformations has been to use power—through theories, concepts and material resources of experts—to rescue or save other people from the life they have been experiencing. . . . [We] question this political process. . . . Instead we offer the hypothesis that consultancy and action-research when practiced at their best, encourages in people the "politics of revelation". . . . Revelation can have many sources. An unconscious source is that of dreaming.

A 1992 workshop that I facilitated with the assistance of a colleague, David Horton, provided an unexpected opportunity to experiment with the discovery of the social dreaming matrix. The staff member who approached me to lead the workshop said that the request was on behalf of students who were in the final year of their training course in one of the helping professions. They now wanted an introduction to psychoanalytic and group dynamic concepts. I decided to eschew formally preparing myself for the course and rely on my previous experience, with the intention of designing and tailoring the workshop with the students as part of the content and process of the weekend itself. I also had easy access to various references and materials that might become relevant. When I met the group (about twenty students, together with one of their tutors), I discovered that their interest in psychoanalytic concepts was both limited and ambivalent, but they wanted to learn more about group dynamics, and that their generally preferred way of learning was "experiential". We then agreed a flexible programme of the action–re-view type, and for the next session I introduced a participative task, which while it permitted the members to reveal as little about themselves as they considered appropriate, did involve them in the process of applying their capacity for observation and imagination, as well as putting them in touch directly with some of the projections and transference dynamics that emerged. The group engaged actively in the task, and, with my facilitation, then decided on the way in which we would use our next session, stemming from their observation of the kinds of ways in which the participation of some of the men differed from that of some of the women.

In the afternoon, I made use of some video vignettes, which again, via the interactions that were generated, manifested group dynamic processes that were then highlighted. For example, we observed a group pressure towards conformity of response, and how anxious a member of the group might feel about introducing a new way of looking at things.

There were also some expressions of anger and frustration with what we were doing and the way we were going about things. I took the opportunity to suggest that these feelings might relate to the group's irritation with me for not being more active in teaching them, and I suggested that this might also be a here-and-now manifestation of their "dependency", which might be blocking a more creative use of our workshop time. At that point, the group seemed to become aware of a total group process for the first time. They responded to this realization by tending to become more autonomous and lively in their participation.

In the course of our ensuing dialogue, I referred to the value of dreams as illuminating aspects of experience which were not already conscious. I thought little more of this until the end of the day, when I suggested as part of my closing remarks that they might keep in mind the possibility of overnight dreams.

That evening, when I reflected on the day's work, I discovered in my mind a picture of the group as being somewhat stylized. For example, I recalled that there were those who spoke a lot and those who said very little, and two or three of the latter group seemed relatively uninvolved in what we were doing. Further-more, those who spoke frequently tended to do so in individually typical ways: one stressing feelings, another ideas, another tending to play devil's advocate, a fourth always looking only at me when-ever she spoke, a fifth expressing confusion, and so on. Although the participation in general was active and engaging, there were indications of underlying tensions in the group, as evidenced by the way in which the group usually ignored communications com-ing from particular individuals, whose words were left to fade away like the ripples generated by pebbles dropped into a still pond. I was reminded of the psychology laboratory demonstration in which students agree or disagree with quotations presented to them, not so much according to the content but in line with the reputation of the person who is supposedly being quoted. I also recalled that one of the students had mentioned in passing that she had ceased to feel accepted by the group following an important development in her life some months ago, and that she, in turn, felt rejecting of the group.

When we assembled the next morning, I was uncertain how to begin and, having communicated this, decided to remain silent for a while to see what initiatives might also come from the rest of the group. This silence continued for five minutes or so, interrupted by late arrivals, and a message of apology from one member who would not be joining us. The last member to arrive late in the still-silent group asked immediately on sitting down whether she had been the only one to have had an overnight dream. We then discovered, to our surprise, that all but two of those present had dreamed the previous night. After a short discussion, we agreed to see what we could learn from these dream experiences. Lawrence (1991), in his account of the dream matrix, recommends sitting in a snowflake pattern, and we discovered how to do this after some trial and error. We were then so arranged that we were each able to see most of the rest of the group without facing anyone else directly.

I introduced the dream-sharing session by suggesting that we did not offer associations to our own dreams, but only to the dreams of others, and that we might also offer our own dreams as a response to someone else's.

My memory of the session that followed was of being transported into a very different group experience from that of the previous day. The group process followed no obvious logic or cohesion, yet somehow had an inspiring sense of wholeness and rhythm—the nearest analogy I can think of is when musicians become engrossed in a session of improvisation. Everyone spoke, and there was a great deal of spontaneity. We uncovered and produced a collage of dreams and associations, during which one of the two people who said that they had not dreamed the night before, suddenly recalled the content of the dream she had dreamed after all. Dreams and images of all kinds abounded, quite a few relating to travel and discovery. The only student not to have had an overnight dream later shared a dream of the night prior to the workshop, which she felt also belonged in our dream matrix. A recurrent theme was of a journey, with individuals specifying many different means of transport and locomotion. A building (house, cottage, church, houseboat) was also a recurrent structure.

The whole experience was a revelation. It was both like children producing spontaneous art and like adults expressing interest and joining in the artwork itself. As I was writing up this account, I received a copy of the journal *Free Associations* in the post, and I was riveted by a paper by David Armstrong (on the psychoanalytic movement) in which he referred to the "workgroup" as an "arena for transformations"; to a group's capacity for "serious play" and "those moments . . . when people are able to associate to each other's material without an irritable preoccupation with ownership and without recourse to a prescriptive idea of 'relevance'" (Armstrong, 1992, p. 277). These words ring true in relation to the session that I am trying to describe. The surprising impact of this session was experienced by all present and reflected in a changed group atmosphere for the rest of the workshop.

When we reassembled in our circle to review our dream session, communication flowed more easily, and the group spontaneously found itself addressing unfinished business relating to its own history, specifically about previous group responses to certain known significant personal events that took place during their course. The group also discovered for the first time that these life events were meaningfully connected and had powerful emotional connotations for all present.

Later that day, one of the members chose to present her own work for "supervision", and the group responded in something of the spirit of the dream matrix, bringing in aspects of their own work and allowing themselves to respond freely and creatively in a way that was enriching for all.

It is difficult to convey the way in which this atmosphere was qualitatively different from my familiar experience as either supervisee or supervisor, and it seems lame to instance the fact of one person even discovering and communicating a creative link between the cries of the gulls, which we heard outside the window, and aspects of the work about which the presenter was telling us.

Another way of putting it is to say that for the first time people seemed free to draw on rich and varied aspects of their life's experience: their interests, pastimes, previous jobs, fantasies, spiritual values, and so on, over and above their role as students. Here are some quotations from three people who wrote to me afterwards:

"By the latter part of Sunday afternoon, the group had gained much confidence, particularly in the dream session."

"[After the dream session] I felt acknowledged by [my group, in relation to events earlier in the course]. I . . . got deep into my feelings and felt able to share a lot of that."

"What always stands out for me when I consider the weekend is the group dreaming. I felt that we, not I, shared on a level wholly different to what we are used to. This was apparent the next day when the group was still very 'bonded' and mellow, as was remarked upon by group members who weren't there at our weekend. . . . This also helped to clarify aspects of the group's identity and process, aspects we are still exploring much later . . . the most important thing was the shared feeling which united us in a new way, and I feel a very important one for all its intangibility. . . . We're grateful you took the risk of trying that with us."

To return to the beginning of this chapter: I am not trying to "promote" working with dreams as an educational tool, recognizing that the workshop I described may be a function of unusual circumstances. Furthermore, I am mindful of the way in which what starts out as a good idea may in some situations be either dangerous to use or vulnerable to smothering or tyrannical institutionalizing processes. What I would much rather do is invite consideration of carefully including work with dreams as relevant to developmental opportunities in "educational" as well as "therapeutic" settings.

CHAPTER THREE

Vision in organizational life

Kenneth Eisold

I n the New Testament, it is reported that when Jesus went into
the wilderness to prepare for his mission as a prophet, Satan
approached him. Outlining one possible version of the future,
Satan offered him a loaf of bread: he could secure him against the
threat of hunger. Failing that, he then suggested Jesus provokes
God into a miraculous intervention: if he threw himself off the
pinnacle of the temple in Jerusalem, God would have to send his
angels to save him. In other words, Satan could secure a bond with
his omnipotent father. Finally, on the mountaintop, Satan pointed
out the worldly power and riches that could be his if he agreed to
rule the world. This is known as the temptation of Christ.

We can look at these temptations as dreams or versions of
possible futures that Jesus had to confront before he could passion-
ately engage the career or the mission that now, in retrospect,
seems inevitably his. First of all, they represent levels of ambition:
from the wish for bodily security (the loaf of bread), to the wish to
satisfy a deep personal longing (being rescued from a fall by his
father), to the wish to find one's place in the widest possible world.
Secondly, and more importantly, they represent the familiar: each

temptation recycles elements of the past into a view of the future. Jesus knew what it was like to have his hunger satisfied, to please his father, to exert power over others. Satan said, in effect, that he could make the future look like the past writ large.

I want to make a distinction between visions and dreams. Dreams, like temptations, present us with versions of what we already know; they set before us goals that restate the past. This is no insignificant or unworthy achievement, I believe, as our wishes and our needs have to be continually restated and adapted to changing circumstances. But visions—if we are fortunate enough to have them—suggest what we don't know. They point the way to futures we do not know and have not imagined.

Much of life is repetitive and familiar, and, even when it is not as familiar as we might like it to be, it is part of our work to make it so, to reduce it to recognizable and usable terms. In open systems theory, for example, for "inputs" to come across the boundary and become available as "throughputs" and, ultimately, "exports", they have to fit certain standard requirements. Whether they are pieces of fruit for a canning factory, barrels of oil for a refinery, or students in an elementary school, variations are not particularly desirable. The teacher who imagines capable and well-behaved pupils has an easier time drawing up lesson plans. The canning factory manager can be forgiven if he dreams of endless lines of perfectly formed pears.

Even managers standing at the boundaries of their organizations understandably are looking for the familiar: new sources of fruit or oil, new markets, but the new should be as much as possible like the old. It should be reliable, predictable. Principals are looking for good teachers and seeking out stable and smoothly functioning relationships with families in the community. There is nothing wrong with that.

Dreams guide us in this quest for the recognizable. They literally scan the horizons of our daily worlds, seeking to match up seemingly unfamiliar and disturbing elements in our experience with familiar elements from the past. In this, they follow what appears to be the guiding principle in all forms of perception: our senses constantly search our environments to confirm the existence of the familiar. We notice the unfamiliar because it does not fit, because it presents us with the problem of finding the categories

within which we can fold it away and so put the potential distur-
bance it represents to rest. We literally do not see the new until we
develop the categories we need to grasp its difference from what
we already know.

It is when the familiar no longer works for us that we are
forced to seek out what we do not know or cannot understand.
That is where the need for vision arises. I am trying to be precise
about this and modest. Most of the time we need good, clear work-
able extrapolations of past experience into the future, solid
statistical analyses, simple predictions. But sometimes we need
more than that. When the present is rapidly shifting and complex,
the future is not easily discernible. We lose our way. We need to
see what can't be seen.

These thoughts arise for me out of my experience with social
dreaming, a set of techniques for learning being developed by
Lawrence to help us see our way into what we do not understand.
At the heart of his work is the notion of the "matrix", the gathering
together of those who dream and share their dreams. The social
dreaming matrix is not a group—or, better yet, it aspires not to be
a group in the sense that we know groups. That is, it is a gathering
of those who share and gradually seek to interpenetrate each
other's unconscious experience. The matrix thus seeks to transcend
the ordinary defensive manoeuvres, such as the basic assumptions,
which in our understanding typically form the internal or unconscious cohesiveness of group life. By setting the task of unconscious
collaboration, the matrix aspires to by-pass the unconscious strategies that establish group cohesiveness in terms of roles and the
search for security.

But dreams—even the dreams that arise in a matrix—are only
a recycling of the past, as I just suggested. More accurately, they
are efforts to take disturbing bits of experience that do not fit into
the habitual patterns and categories that we carry around in our
cognitive apparatus and make them fit by finding the archaic patterns where they will fit. Ultimately, as I suggested in my reference
to the temptation of Jesus, they are ways in which we bend what is
potentially upsetting, unfamiliar, and new into what we can recognize. But—and this is the important point—they occur on the
frontier of the familiar; they are occasioned by disturbing experiences that do not readily fit into familiar patterns. Or they may be

occasioned by intriguing or powerful experiences where the usual patterns of recognition do not suffice. So just as a dream can be taken to the psychoanalytic setting and deconstructed into clues about the patient's experience that he or she is unwilling or unable to attend to, so dreams can be brought to the matrix and be subject to the associations and the dreams of others. In this way, the clues that they contain about the disturbingly unfamiliar, rather than becoming folded back into the repetitions of the past, can become enlarged and amplified. Common elements of disturbing experience in the social field can become recognized and links can be established. Gradually, unfamiliar patterns, new configurations, unexpected meanings can be revealed. In short, a process can be set in motion in which the dream leads to vision.

Lawrence has run a number of social dreaming programmes around the world, and the New York Center of the A. K. Rice Institute has had the good fortune of sponsoring three of them. I want at this point to talk about the use of social dreaming as an action-research project, an effort to use the technique of social dreaming specifically to intervene in an organization in order to facilitate the process of clarifying its vision. The design that was developed was a series of matrices alternating with "Project Groups", groups that would seek explicitly to focus on issues in the organization. The primary task of the project groups was stated as follows: "To interpret the state of this institution using information derived from the matrices and members' own experience in the institution." The organization into which the intervention took place was the Organizational Development and Consultation Programme at the William Alanson White Institute (WAWI), a programme run by Larry Gould, Kathy White, and myself. In effect, we were inviting Lawrence and his staff to come into our institution and test out social dreaming as an action research tool. That had never been done before. We also wanted—and expected—to gain from the revelations that it would give rise to.

In order to try to give some sense of how it actually worked, I would like to isolate one central theme that emerged in the matrices and try to describe how it got worked in the project groups: the theme of terrorism. It first emerged explicitly in the fourth social dreaming matrix, SDM4. A second-year student in the programme, a young married woman, reported the following dream: *"I am in my house, giving lunch to my son. For a couple of days in a row, terrorists had come into the neighbourhood. I went to a friend whose husband is an expert and said I'm ready to have a gun. Then, suddenly, out the window someone is running by with an Uzi. It's unclear if the person is providing protection or is a terrorist.*" Following this, another student reported a dream of *being in Germany with her godson and being subject to sexual harassment in the street.* Shortly afterwards, the following dream was reported by another female student, a dream that, she said, closely followed a real experience. "*We are living in a Detroit enclave; my son* [6 years old at the time] *is the only non-black child in his class. He is active and he spoke up in class. The school called: he was taken to the principal's office and flogged, bruised all over his butt. The principal is a black male. I am enraged that a poor white boy is flogged by a black male and there is no recourse in the system.*"

In retrospect, it is possible to see that the eruption of this theme in SDM4 was prefigured in earlier matrices. In the SDM1, a student reported a dream in which *he was compelled by a disembodied voice to perform an autopsy without any previous experience*—what seemed a clear reference to the programme's task of training students to perform analytic interventions. In SDM2, one dream by a member of the faculty included the thought, as the dreamer was walking the streets of Harlem, "*The trick to survival is not to look scared.*" Another dream referred to *a school librarian disclaiming any responsibility for controlling the fighting between two students,* and a third dream referred to a *sadistic music teacher teaching a circus-like, "trivial" march.* Again, authority figures were irresponsible or sadistic. The third matrix, SDM3, contained two dreams referring to surveillance: in one, *the toiling, dirty Indian masses were being observed as though by tourists;* as one of the consultants pointed out, Wilfred Bion was born in India and A. K. Rice did his pioneering work consulting to textile mills there as well. The other dream involved *faceless travellers on a train, invisible and naked, striving not to be seen or noticed but nevertheless betraying their presence to each other.*

The project group immediately following SDM4 began with an intense discussion of the meaning of terrorism in the context of the programme. The hypotheses generated had to do, largely, with paranoid mechanisms. Our sophisticated students hypothesized that hatred and aggression were being projected onto leadership figures in the programme, figures that should be providing protection (like the principal or, possibly, the neighbourhood guards in the first dream) but instead were experienced as terrorizing. This line of reasoning developed into some very good work that had to do with uncovering the terrifying nature of the work that our students are being trained to do. The work is terrifying because it is so complex and difficult: one does not really know how to negotiate a consultation contract with a particular client—the faculty has said, a number of times—until the consultation is virtually finished. But the work is also terrifying because one is tapping into an organization filled with terror: it is like intervening in a domestic fight where members are both terrorizing and terrorized, ready to project each aspect onto the intruding consultant.

This line of reasoning went, then, towards interpreting the terrorism—or sadism—of authority figures as projections onto them by terrorized students, consultants in training, who were feeling insufficiently protected and enraged by the nature of the task that they were confronted with.

This, in turn, led to a discussion of unmet dependency needs of students in the programme. One set of hypotheses came up having to do with the perception on the part of the students that the faculty are so tightly paired up with each other or so banded together (as in a male brotherhood) that there is no place for students to aspire to be in relation to them. Another line of discussion had to do with the failure of the faculty to provide structures in which students can seek help or reassurance for their dependency needs or their more realistic fears of incompetence. A hypothesis was then advanced that the faculty wished for the students to fail—a hypothesis that seems to parallel explicitly the terrorist dreams of the matrix, in which protectors become persecutors. Indeed, it seemed clear that without the prompting of the dream from the matrix, it was unlikely that the direct statement—or accusation—could have been made.

I responded, at this point, defensively. Consciously, I was not aware of feeling guilty of—and therefore defensive about—wishing the students to fail. But I was feeling literally frightened and resentful at the prospect of having to provide "structures" for the dependency needs of students. I became angry at what I perceived as yet another demand and blurted out something about my incredulity and fear that more could be expected of us. This put me in touch with the fact that I have felt this way before in the programme, and I found myself, somewhat to my own surprise, speaking of containing feelings of being overwhelmed and needing to control demands upon my time and my emotions. I was then able to speak about my resistance to acknowledging these needs and my becoming, at moments, grudging and sadistic in parrying demands for attention and reassurance. At this time, Larry Gould, in response to what appeared to be genuine anxiety and dismay on the part of students, offered the thought that he and the other members of the faculty had been somewhat grandiose in underestimating the extent of the demands that the programme placed upon them. He conjectured that, had the faculty known how complex and intense the demands upon us in running the programme were to be, we would probably never have undertaken it in the first place—though he added that it was also stimulating and gratifying beyond our expectations. I thoroughly agreed with his comments and experienced gratitude and relief at acknowledging the point.

This was an intense and crucial moment in the project group: an emotional truth in the relatedness between students and faculty was exposed. Their terror could now be seen as anxiety driven to desperation by the faculty's unwillingness to recognize it; in turn, the faculty could be seen as struggling to contain the sense of being overwhelmed. The trick to the faculty's survival seemed to lie in "not looking scared", as one dreamer put it.

The theme of terrorism, however, remained—though it underwent a transformation. In SDM5, a student reported a dream in which *her white van was stolen*; in a second dream, a student in the course of a consulting project *was driving a white van*. (Recall that the programme is at the White Institute.) A third dream involved *a motorcade stopped because of a bomb threat, but the dreamer notices that everyone is standing next to their stopped cars as if convinced that the bomb would be found before it went off.*

In SDM6, a student reported the following dream: "*I had felt cut off. I am small, in a forest, wooded with high trees, and I needed to find a safe place. I find Dr. Doolittle—it is 'x'* [a fellow student, a female psychoanalyst]. *He took me by the hand, and took me to a safe place, a gingerbread house, dripping with sugar and all sorts of candies. It was beautiful. Yet the edges of the house were sharp, spoke-like. It glowed weirdly; it was radioactive. I felt betrayed."*

The project group meetings that followed these matrices began with a discussion of some of the more grandiose or messianic ideas about the programme that have been put forth by faculty and students alike. Larry Gould said that he would be happy if the programme just succeeded in developing some consulting skills in its participants, and that was likened to a "blue-collar" ambition. This led to a more far-reaching discussion trying to define what, after all, the primary task of the programme was.

Interestingly, the discussion came around to the dream reported in SDM4, in which *"a poor white boy was flogged by a black man and there was no recourse in the system"*. What was seen as significant now was the fact that the woman reporting the dream, which she said was based on an actual incident involving her son, was Hispanic. Why would a Hispanic woman refer to her son as "a poor white boy"? In then trying to link this discussion with the earlier focus on ambiguity about the programme's primary task, two points emerged. The first had to do with the difficulty of identifying oneself in a context in which one did not know what one belonged to. Just as there was ambiguity for the mother about which community she belonged to, there was ambiguity for all the programme participants about how they belonged to the programme so long as the essential purpose of the programme remained unclear. Retrospectively, we can see this point reflected in the dreams about the white vans, stolen or lost en route to a consultation: where is this programme going? to whom does it belong? The second point that emerged from the discussion about this dream had to do with an underlying or covert purpose in the programme which began to emerge: perhaps participants and faculty too are seeking out a holding environment in which their organizational dilemmas and conflicts will be understood and repaired. To put it bluntly, the underlying confusion about primary task was this: do we teach a skill or do we repair and restore persons in roles?

Suddenly, the dream about Dr. Doolittle and the radioactive gingerbread house made a lot more sense. On one level, clearly, it represented the wish to be saved; but on another, it was saying something about illusory or deceptive appearances. What is this gingerbread house, and who is the psychoanalytic Dr. Doolittle? What, after all, does he do, apart from talk to the animals and fix them up?

The final matrix—the event with which the entire intervention came to an end—included a dream about *a hit-and-run incident,* which alluded to the assassination of John F. Kennedy, *and the search for a witness driving a white car with diplomatic plates from a West African country.* There was a dream fragment about *being stuck on about the ninetieth floor of a World Trade Center tower after the bombing; a consultant was there whose job was to help the dreamer get information that he needed, but neither the student nor the consultant could get out.* The final two dreams were about deformed children. In the first one, *the child seemed to have an excess layer of skin,* but the point of the dream was *that the dreamer found he could love the child anyway.* In the second dream, *the dreamer was looking at a photograph of two children with deformed heads, a niece and a nephew, observed by three others, and the question was "Should I keep the picture?" The answer in the dream was "yes",* but she thought it too bad that the father, *now 80 or 85, had abused his children.*

I think it is possible to see in all of these final dreams the issue of identity: the unknown driver of the white car who witnessed the event, the consultant who couldn't help, the deformed children—all these figures represent unrealized identities. The theme of terror and terrorism is still there in the incident on the grassy knoll, the bomb at the World Trade Centre, the abuse of children. But the tone is muted and complex; the dreamer feels the suffering of the children but neither casts them away nor rejects those who may have abused them. More importantly, some central uncomfortable but vital truths have become very clear about the programme. One has to do with the high level of anxiety in the students in approaching the work and the faculty's unwillingness to recognize that level of anxiety as they struggle to keep the work going. The second has to do with the lack of clarity about the primary task, the ambiguity about being a training programme or a place of repair for organizational role casualties. In effect, what are the professional identities that the programme is in the process of attempting to create?

What does this have to do with vision? The social dreaming intervention left us with essential insights about our dilemmas, insights that have now allowed us to set our agenda for future work on our design and our mission. It did not provide answers. The future is still opaque. But our past is far clearer than it ever was, so clear that we ignore what it tells us at our peril.

Last year, at the end of the social dreaming programme in New York, my final dream was of *being invited by Lawrence to join him in a horse-and-buggy sightseeing tour of Manhattan, but to my surprise when he gave me a hand up it was to sit next to him in the front seat looking backwards*. It was perfectly clear to me in reporting the dream that this was the nature of vision, seeing what we can not know. Others, too, had similar dreams of running or walking backwards. The technique seems old-fashioned, the process clumsy; moreover, it is profoundly disconcerting to give up knowing what one thinks one knows.

There is a tradition in religious thought about the connection between vision and blindness. Paul had to be struck blind and dumb by lightning on the road to Damascus to be enlightened. Oedipus, like Tiresias, becomes wise when he loses his sight. In the dark night of the soul does the truth become revealed.

Others may see into the future with compelling insights and visions. Reality may be starkly delineated. Those of us groping our way forward without seeing clearly where we are going might consider pooling our dreams.

CHAPTER FOUR

The use of dreams
in systems-centred theory

Thomas A. Michael

T here are two interests that I would like to try to deal with in this chapter. The first is my fascination with the concept of social dreaming as it has been developed over the past decade; the second is systems-centred theory. Specifically, I hope to show how the use of social dreaming can become a legitimate part of systems-centred work.

In a systems-centred group, care is taken to ensure that participants remain in the here-and-now. A dream, of course, takes one out of the present boundaries of time and space. The issue is how to bring such an experience across the boundaries into the group.

I begin with a brief description of what social dreaming is and what one hopes to accomplish by engaging in it. Then I give an account of a dream that was recounted at a systems-centred group meeting, and I show how it was used to further the work of the group.

Social dreaming

It has been suggested that dreams may be understood not only as representations of individual difficulties, but also as representations of beliefs about organizations and communities; "the dream that is offered in a group which is beyond the individual dreamer's personal life and which speaks to the life of the group" (Lawrence, 1991). A keystone of this approach which has great resonance for me is that there is a need for a "politics of revelation" as opposed to a "politics of salvation" (Lawrence, 1994). That is to say, the usual relationship between client and consultant is that of "salvation": one has some sort of trouble, seeks out an expert, and the expert, on the basis of specialized knowledge, diagnoses the trouble and gives directions on the best way to solve it. It is the classic relationship between doctor and patient, but it may also be found between computer expert and intimidated user, accountant and business owner, clergy and congregant, pollster and politician. It is Lawrence's contention, however, that in the modern, turbulent world, both the saviour and supplicant are in need of a collaborative approach to a new understanding of what is needed. This is the politic of revelation, where the new knowledge has to be entertained from wherever it may come.

I do not necessarily believe that dreams predict the future. I do believe that they enable us to be more in touch with what is already happening but about which we are not yet conscious, much as Bollas has formulated the idea of the "unthought known" (Bollas, 1987). It may be that, as Marshall McLuhan said thirty years ago, we modern humans go though life looking through a rear-view mirror. The artist, according to McLuhan (1967), is one who is able to look *around* rather than look back and thus appears to the rest of us to be a visionary. The Book of Revelation in the New Testament, usually considered to be prophesies of the future, was originally presented as an apocalypse, an uncovering. So dreams enable us to look around.

When a dream is offered in a social dreaming programme, participants are free to respond in many ways. Participants are seated irregularly, in what is called a matrix, in order to minimize group dynamic effects. Some may give an interpretation, others an association, others a dream of their own that seems to be related. Often, a dream matrix will be the recounting of dreams with hardly any other content, and the result is to be used by participants in ways that they are free to choose. Consultants to the matrix attempt to "be available for thought" and to notice themes that may have escaped the attention of participants. The outcome often appears to be a sharing of experience at a deep level. Often, this sharing can be expressed as a hypothesis about the group, community, or society.

The dream in the group

With this background, I will proceed to relate a social dream that was presented in the course of a group that I conducted. I had just returned from attendance at a social dreaming programme and was beginning a group session with students in a pastoral counselling training programme. The group consisted of six members in their second year of a three-year course. The group was in the spring of its second term and had been meeting with me since the beginning of its first year. The stated purposes of the group, which met bi-weekly during the term, were to provide mutual support for the members as they engaged in the programme and to teach them the elements of group dynamics. One condition of my appointment to lead the group was that, as an outsider to the staff of the institute, I would be expected not to share information about the group or its members with the staff. I should add that I was friends with two members of the senior staff, and that I had served briefly on the board of directors of the institute several years earlier. I was thus familiar with some of the history and organizational issues of the institute.

I began the group session by asking if there were distractions that were keeping members' energy and attention from attending to the here-and-now reality of the group. After several members had briefly described their distractions and their feelings, and had brought those feelings into the meeting, the group became silent. I sat there wishing that I could ask whether anyone had had any good dreams. However, since a standard of systems-centred groups is to keep the experience in the here-and-now, I chose to remain silent.

At that moment "Alice" (I have changed names of members) said, "I had a dream last night that I believe has something to do with this group." She then related a dream in which *she was in a desert in a foreign country attending the funeral of a young girl. The mourners were wrapped in white robes in the style of nomads so that only their faces could be seen. The dead girl was not in a coffin but was wrapped in strips of grave cloths (swaddling clothes). The dreamer looked at the face of the girl and was certain that she was not dead. She whispered to the person beside her: "You know, she really doesn't look dead to me." When she was assured quickly that the child was dead, the funeral proceeded. She thought, "Well, I'm not an expert on death, I'm in a foreign country, and I don't know the customs here. Perhaps she really is dead. I had better keep quiet." In the dream, Alice felt afraid. The child was buried in a deep hole in the sand and the funeral continued. As it was concluding the sand began to move and the small body wriggled up through the sand and sat up.* At that point the dream ended.

Alice continued by relating her dream to events of the day. She was feeling quite discouraged, in part because an interview related to her certification examination had not gone well (even though she had passed), and in part because it was the beginning of Lent, which was a particularly busy time for pastors (she was part-time pastor in a parish, in addition to her training and counselling). She added that she thought she needed to read a then best-selling book called *Women Who Run with Wolves*.

She then began to make some interpretations about the dream for herself, and at that point I chose to intervene. One choice of intervention could have been to treat the experience as a distraction, since it often happens that a member may discover a distraction after the fact. Instead, I chose to intervene by asking: "Does that dream have a subgroup?" The criterion for membership in a functional subgroup is that a member has the experience of "resonance", a basic apprehension aroused by the experience of another.

Two of the six, "Bradley" and "Catherine", joined the subgroup, and I invited them to describe their visceral experience of resonance. Catherine sat with slumped shoulders and a drawn face and described a bodily feeling of being weighed down, and of heaviness in her chest. Bradley also felt heavy and empty in his stomach. I asked whether this was a subgroup of those who felt weighed down and buried and whether any of the others felt part of this subgroup. "Dorothy" responded by saying that she was feeling quite different, energized to the point of explosiveness. "Edward" stirred physically at that and added that he was feeling heat in his belly and behind his eyes. I observed that the group had split into two subgroups—the weighed-down subgroup and the energized, exploding subgroup. "Frank" said that he was feeling both discouraged and heavy as well as energized and exploding. I suggested that he choose one of these and join that subgroup. I reminded him that his criterion for choice should be that which would afford him the opportunity to explore what he felt was important for him to keep at that time. I also pointed out that the other subgroup would contain that part of his experience that he would not be exploring. He decided to join the energized, explosive subgroup. I asked the members of that group to contain their experience while the other subgroup worked, and I encouraged them to maintain continual eye contact with one another.

In a systems-centred group, the work is in the here-and-now. In order for that to happen, members need to cross the boundaries of space and time to be fully present. Thus, distractions are to be left outside the boundaries, while the energy is brought across the boundary to the here-and-now. The group is enabled to become the container for all of the experience of its members. This makes it possible for members to explore the most salient part of their experience without loss of another part. To keep an individual from reverting from his member role and thus being lost to the group system, members are encouraged to form a subgroup that contains one part of the experience. They are enabled to do this either by working with other members of the subgroup or by maintaining silent eye contact with members of their subgroup when they are not working; in this way, an individual may escape becoming an identified patient or a scapegoat.

With their agreement, Alice, Bradley, and Catherine began to explore and deepen their experience. Much of this amounted to describing ever more specifically their bodily experience. I encouraged them to allow the feelings to fill their whole selves. There were descriptions of how their arms felt heavy and their legs were tired. They also made associations. Bradley related a fantasy in which he was in a slick, smooth marble crypt. It recalled a dream of his dead father, and he experienced a shuddering feeling of horror. He felt all closed in, calling it claustrophobic. Alice described in a small voice how it was hard to speak out loud. They continued in the experience, but began to have longer and longer periods of silence.

I asked if they would be able to contain their experience and give space for the other subgroup to work. Dorothy began immediately with a description of feeling very hot in her whole body. Her face was flushed. She spoke with force and said that she was feeling angry. Edward responded to that by describing intense explosiveness deep in his belly. He put both hands on his middle and described the heat deep inside. As they continued to resonate and explore, they became aware of great anger and feelings of murderous rage. I encouraged them to maintain contact with one another and to allow themselves to fill up with the rage. Edward identified the target of his rage as the administrators of the programme.

I then announced that the group had come to the time boundary ending the experiential part of the group, and that they could now have the opportunity to process the experience, beginning with surprises and learning, satisfactions and dissatisfactions.

Several of the members expressed surprise at the depth and intensity of their feelings. They were aware of how they had been containing feelings of being both smothered and exploding, and how these were defences against their true feelings of rage and despair. Alice saw herself as not claiming her own voice. Bradley became aware of how he was horrified by his own anger, and of how he sabotaged himself by being compliant and accepting of authority, even dead authority. Dorothy described her determination that this death was not going to happen, and she was energized by a sense of release of life force. She felt herself filled with life writhing, erupting, and coming forth. She felt that she was claiming her life anew. Edward was surprised by his own intensity of anger and how he was keeping it bottled up. I describe his subsequent work later.

Issues of using dreams
in systems-centred groups

I am not a group therapist, but a university teacher in the fields of organizational development and organizational behaviour. My interests lie in the understanding of the psychodynamics of work groups and organizations. Systems-centred groups require that members of the group cross the role boundary from their social or personal selves to their member selves. This means that they must bring any feelings generated by previous experiences into the group as energy available for the here-and-now experience.

Members are encouraged to stay in the here-and-now and to relate their behaviour to what is present. This does, of course, arouse turbulence. In addition, powerful memories of earlier events and experiences can come into play. The dream in this particular case could have been treated as a there-and-then experience. One option could have been to treat it as a distraction and to encourage Alice to give the briefest of descriptions and concentrate on bringing the accompanying feeling state into the group. I chose to consider the dream as belonging to the group (I must acknowledge that there was an element of experimentation in my choice).

Had the dream been considered to be an event from the past, the other members of the group could have joined Alice in attempting to interpret the meaning of the dream as she had begun to do. This might have led to her becoming an "identified patient". However, by treating the dream as a present experience, Alice was enabled to identify her own feeling state, and others were able to determine their own resonance to that. "Resonance is the signal that there is an open communication between the primary apprehensive and secondary comprehensive selves" (Agazarian, 1993). When others are prevented from identifying a patient, they are brought back to their own experience rather than projecting it onto another.

> Spontaneous resonance and deepening of the experience is considered to be a healing activity. Members are also encouraged to allow themselves to fill up with the experience of the feelings as they have them, and to see whether or not the explanation of the experience is in reality the experience that

they "think" or "say" it is. Often, of course, it is not! For example, members are almost always surprised to find that the experience of anger is often, in fact, exciting, freeing and empowering, and it is the way they think about it that makes it unpleasant. This often also means that members recognize how much of their emotion is generated by their defences against their primary experience rather than by the primary experience itself. [Agazarian, 1993]

Bradley's explanation of his feeling as claustrophobic was an example of a defence. By framing the feeling, giving it a name, he in effect distanced himself from that feeling, if only for a moment. Likewise, Frank's ambivalence, in which he said he felt partly smothered and partly explosive, may have been a defence against exploring either experience deeply. Since a defence is a traditional way of avoiding a present reality, it diverts energy that a living human system could use to reach its goals. Instead of analysing defences, a systems-centred approach attempts to get to the feelings that are being defended against.

There are similarities between systems-centred theory and social dreaming. Treating a dream as a social phenomenon parallels the idea that "in a systems-centred group, the basic unit is not the individual member, but the sub-group" (Agazarian, 1994). Encouraging members of a social dreaming matrix to respond to the dream is similar to the experience of resonance. Participants in social dreaming programmes have had the uncanny experience of hearing their own dreams related by others ("You had my dream!") and of having their own dreams taken up by the matrix in such a way that they are no longer experienced as being their own possession. By contrast, a dream in a traditional group-therapy group is usually treated as the possession of one individual.

There is a significant difference between the approach of social dreaming and systems-centred theory in the attitude towards the group. Social dreaming is conducted in a matrix, in which members are spaced irregularly with little opportunity for eye contact. The stated purpose of this arrangement is to minimize the effects of group dynamics, which is always in a circle to maximize eye contact, and to provide a container for members to be equally available for thought. This contrasts with systems-centred theory

in that group development is an important ingredient in understanding the experience. In both cases, unlike psychodynamic
groups, the group is not left to develop naturally. Instead, certain
behaviours are encouraged and others discouraged.

Since my field is organizational development, a major interest
for me is the issue raised by the emphasis upon here-and-now
experience as it relates to the placement of the group within its
organizational context. In this case, the group was part of a pastoral counselling institute. It is my experience that issues of govern-
ance and administration in the parent body could not fail to have
some effect upon the group. I believe that this should be taken into
consideration when therapy groups are conducted in an in-patient
setting, or in the context of training for students who are enrolled
in the sponsoring organization. Eisold (1994) has described the role
of splits in psychoanalytic groups and the effect that these splits
have had upon the development of competing theories. (I believe
that this illustrates the wisdom of Yvonne Agazarian's insistence
that a systems-centred theory organization should be developed in
a manner consistent with the theory that underlies its practice.)

I had some previous knowledge of the difficulties that the institute faced in management and finances. I had the sense throughout
the life of the group that I could get at least a glimpse of the problems of the institute by being open to the experience of the group
meetings. Braxton and Klein (1996) have shown how relationships
between consultant and client parallel the relationships in the
client organization. In just the same way as members of the group
were smothering their anger, the administrators were smothering
their conflicts until they could work out their administrative and
financial problems, not expressing their anger. I believe that this
illustrates the principle of isomorphy.

In the group, Edward identified one of the administrators as
the target of his anger. This might have been seen as a retreat out
of the group, and as avoidance of anger towards me as the authority in the group. I can assure you that I certainly had been, and
would later be, a container of unacceptable parts of the group and
hated for it. Why this did not seem to be the case here is because
the group had moved into the second phase of development, having worked through the first phase of flight/fight. I believe that the

group was in a transitional phase, moving towards maturity. Thus, the members were able to identify and direct their anger at the administrators of the program rather than at me.

This assessment is borne out by the actions that Edward undertook after the experience in the group. He had been behaving in a compliant manner towards his supervisor and the director of training, even though he had several grievances. He subsequently reported to me (a year later) that his behaviour had been intensified by the fact that his wife had had two miscarriages, and they were so discouraged that they were at the point of not trying again to conceive. He was generally angry.

After this group, he decided to leave the programme. He focused his anger towards the director of training and his clinical supervisor. In his report of these events, he quoted Martin Luther King: "Not everything that is faced can be changed, but nothing can be changed until it is faced." He subsequently enrolled in another programme and successfully completed it (and it may not be coincidental that he and his wife were able to have another child).

Conclusion

My purpose here has been to examine how a dream can become a vital route to group experience. As a result, I have related my dreams in five-day, systems-centred theory training events, and the dreams appeared to work as a request for a subgroup with good effect. I intend to continue exploring how they may be developed. I feel as though I am on the edge of the unknown, both in social dreaming and in systems-centred theory. It is a lively and enlivening place to be.

CHAPTER FIVE

The social dreaming matrix

Peter Tatham and Helen Morgan

T he application of social dreaming to Jungian thought has opened exciting possibilities. Jung saw the dream as a spontaneous, creative expression of the unconscious psyche which arose to comment upon, and compensate for, deficiencies in any conscious situation. Since archetypal theory implies that dreams can be seen also from a collective angle, dreaming might be "intending" to inform and transform the social and political context of the dreamer as well as the personal situation. As individuals of the late twentieth century, we dream within a context that is in a state of flux. Increased communications mean that the conscious mind is bombarded with images reflecting the divisions, conflicts, and uncertainties of our world. In our daily work as analysts, we are involved in exploration of the dream as it relates to the personal unconscious of the individual as well as the connection to an archetypal, collective aspect. The social dreaming matrix provides a possible arena within which that collective angle might have expression.

We saw the Thirteenth International Congress for Analytical Psychology, in Zurich, 1995, as an arena for analysts familiar with the concept of the collective to attend to the unconscious processes that might occur within those present. People came to Zurich, in middle Europe, from all corners of the globe, at a time approaching the end of the millennium. For five days we would listen, speak, think, and discuss. We would also dream. We wondered what dreams we would experience there and what those dreams might tell us about the nature of the collective context in which we found ourselves. Might those dreams, if explored from the perspective of the social rather than the personal, shed light on the open questions with which we are faced and which were to be the theme of the conference? The social dreaming matrix was a means of investigating these questions.

In the social dreaming matrix participants met to share their dreams. The primary task of the event was to associate to one's own and others' dreams that were made available to the matrix, so as to make links and find connections. It was not necessary to bring a dream to take part; neither was it necessary to participate every day. There were at least eighty participants every morning.

The chairs were set out in the form of a spiral or a snowflake. It was not a circle, and the concerns were not those of group work. The door was left open, and people could enter at any time during the hour. Thus, while the time and space for the event were established, the individual relationship to boundaries was not the focus. Nor were the usual transference issues. As conveners, our roles were to hold time and task boundaries, to record the dreams presented, and to comment on themes where it seemed helpful. We gave attention to the dream and to thinking about the images presented.

While it is not possible in a short space to explore the content of the dreams presented, certain themes emerged that related to the task and context of the Congress itself. Ancestors and parents appeared in the dream images, and associations to our struggles to find an appropriate relationship to our theory parents were made.

The death of Jung was a recurring theme. On the first morning, there was a dream of *a body buried in cement which the dreamer was trying to get rid of, but the body kept re-emerging*. Everyone was upset and tried to hide it. Associations centred around the image of the body of Jung that seems to refuse to die. Do we have to find a way of finally burying this body? Does not the dream also pose the question of how we can set Jung free?

There were also dreams of siblings, cousins, and second cousins. If we look at analytical psychology on a generational basis, these dream images could be thought of as posing the question of how we talk to each other when we are even more distantly related than second cousins. How do we retain a sense of family across the continents, both geographic and philosophical?

The Tower of Babel appeared as a theme in a Congress paper by Kaj Noschis. Prior to this paper, a dream was presented in the matrix of *a mountain with four rocky pinnacles on the top. Within it was a beautiful place, like a Chinese landscape with waterfalls and willow trees. At the bottom of the mountain was a rainforest full of animals and shanty towns.* As these images permeated the matrix, a paradox arose. It is our nature to keep our eye on the top of the mountain, to aspire to the city of God—yet do we not need to attend also to life in the shanty towns at the base if we are to live in the world of humans?

There is the wish to unite to build the City of Humans that is like the City of God, and to speak with one tongue. Yet the reality is that we speak in many tongues. Throughout the Congress, we were listening to papers in four languages; without interpretation, we could not have understood each other. How are we to manage the variety of tongues spoken by the different schools within Jungian thought? In the Tower of Babel story it is God who demolishes the tower and forces diversity of language. While we must work to manage the diversity within our profession, perhaps it is inevitable that we never achieve unity, for this would mean stagnation and hubris—characteristics that the psyche seems to abhor.

Perhaps the power of the matrix is that within it many tongues may be spoken without one having to have authority or power over others. A "multi-verse" rather than a "universe" develops within which a plethora of meanings can co-exist. There is no answer, no "right" interpretation or response. Instead, the matrix offers a container with elastic boundaries that can stretch to take in and hold each new meaning. Again, the dreams conveyed the notion that the direct approach, although appealing, often fails. There were many images of attempts to "get over the top" of hills, slopes, and mountains. Vehicles were unevenly weighted and veered off to one side as they slid back downhill. Banks could be negotiated if the angle of assault was altered. Thus, instead of aspiring to the beauties of the mountaintop, we cannot neglect the places we inhabit down below. While respecting the sacred, its glorification may lead to an inversion into its negative opposite, and the mundane—even the profane—needs attention.

It was not just the plethora of meanings and associations to a particular dream that could be held within the matrix, but the dreams themselves—when seen in relation to each other—asserted plurality. When a dream image arose that looked as if it were leading us in a particular direction, another would come up that implied the opposite. One participant told of a dream in which *a large white bird had to be shot, a necessary act*. In the same session another image was offered where the dreamer was *leaving Zurich and a large white swan came to see her off at the station*. Within two dreams we had the malign and the benign white bird. In the context of a conference entitled "Open Questions", it seemed that the images from the unconscious were determined to keep to this task and not allow us to close down with answers.

Perhaps surprisingly, this was not a frustrating or unrewarding experience. People spoke of a sense of wholeness, of the matrix as a healing experience in contrast to some of the more conflictual, "political" aspects of the Congress. While in many arenas we have to close options by making choices, electing representatives, and deciding policy, perhaps there is also a need for arenas in which we can collaborate in exploring uncertainty and paradox. Because issues of power, authority, and responsibility were not the matters of the matrix, because the role of the dreamer and of the person associating to it is a truly democratic one, the individual is free to engage with others in exploration, and a sense of *communitas* develops. It is not that the matrix avoids the difficulties of human connectedness—the dreams themselves raised some painful themes of shame concerning racism, gender, splits and divisions, political in-fighting within the Congress, shadow, and evil—but people were able to engage with each other to explore such matters around the image of the dream.

The currency of the matrix seems to be paradox. Despite large numbers, participants said that they felt this to be a place where each could be heard. It was a collective experience where not everyone spoke and where often you did not know who was reporting a dream, and yet the individual was not lost. The matrix offered a container that gave a space for the difference of individuality to be "held" by the collective. The "problems" were provided not by the conscious ego but by the images of the dream. The focus was not the individual but the collective. Hence the tensions and clashes between individual egos could be put aside and something more unconscious, more collective had voice. The assumption was that people could manage their experience for themselves, and, indeed, within this large collection of people there were no indications of regressive behaviour—of fight/flight or dependency—that one might expect within such a large group. Rather than feeling denied, individuals felt, on the whole, attended to.

Keats' concept of "negative capability", where questions can be kept open "without any irritable reaching after fact and reason", comes to mind. The matrix does not offer a place where difficult questions can be answered, but it does allow them to be asked. The lesson it may offer at a time when tensions are high is that, instead of directing our energies at finding answers, it may be more helpful to ask what kind of container we need to work in to entertain open questions.

CHAPTER SIX

After Shakespeare—
the language of social dreaming

Francis Oeser

> I wanted a miracle to convince me. But here it is, the only
> possible existing miracle, surrounding me on all sides, and I
> did not even observe it! What greater miracles can there be?
>
> Tolstoi, 1912, p. 34

A residential working conference, "Social Dreaming for the Management of Transformations, The Fourth Programme of Dialogues", was held at Wast Hills House, Birmingham, from 12 to 17 July 1992. Twelve people—French, English, Irish, Scottish, and American—from the professions, business, the Church, and the arts participated.

The core of the conference was the twice-daily, two-hour social dreaming matrix (SDM), and there were ten sessions in all. The operating process of the matrix involved relating dreams, in order to associate to and to interpret their social (not personal) meaning. The assumption is that it is possible to discover links with others' experiences of their world as expressed through dreams and associations, and that in this process of "revelation" lie holistic transformations of the world, with some hope for the future. A summary of the conference and a brief discussion of the diversity of the dreams, their structural relationships and themes, and some possible working tools are contained in *Social Dreaming and Shakespeare* (Oeser, 1992).

Utilizing some of the Shakespearean scholarship, particularly on imagery, word-play, and dramatic structure, we can, firstly, illuminate the transforming relatedness, the "dialogical" processes in the social dreaming matrix—that is, the ways in which the dreams were related and how they invoked succeeding imagery, in the terms set out by Mikhail Bakhtin (Kelly, 1992; Morson & Emerson, 1990).

Secondly, we can exemplify aspects of the "holistic transformations". We are here not involved with psychoanalytic preoccupations, but rather with dramatic and literary language; not with interpretation, but with the forms of expression and the processes which gave the conference its coherence. Furthermore, is the unpremeditated form that evolved similar to the premeditated structure of a play?

So first, an exploration of beginnings: the opening dream of the conference, plus the first dream of another session; then the opening scene of Shakespeare's *King Lear*. Each is a pertinent prelude to the material that follows it. Second, a look at the end of the conference and the end of *The Tragedy of King Lear* (the 1623 version), each a backwards-looking review with tentative expectations for the future.

That both the conference and the play have a dramatic form suggests that we carry within us knowledge and skills that uniquely the social dreaming matrix encourages us to utilize. To have experienced the transformation of the jumble of dreams into such a richly felt whole is to discover hope in an ability to re-make our world more fully whole than seems possible in the rack of the tough everyday.

The first dream

The first dream told in the first matrix session (Dl, SDM1) was:

D1:   *"I am looking out from my home–warehouse, which is ringed with policemen, shoulder-to-shoulder. I say goodbye to home and go down to a seedy kiosk and, "Third Man"–like, into a sewer, and run, run. The chances of escape seem slim. Then caught/caught-up, I am in discussion with another who is going to jail, so is trying to make ordinary financial arrangements (he owes me money!). We agree that I will help him with his management problem, although we are some-how in the same boat."*

The imagery of this dream anticipates many of the themes developed during the ten matrix sessions. Firstly, the paradox of a home–warehouse, which alludes to the ubiquitous homeless with box, blanket, sleeping-bag, cardboard in either hostel or warehouse homes. For as the fool cries, "He that has a house to put his head in has a good head-piece!" (*Lear*, 3.2.25). King Lear stays out in the storm. The dreamer of this first dream runs and runs; his dwelling was a storage-place-become-living-place, as the conference centre became home for its duration, storing not packages or stock but dreamers and consultants. Here is a home's protective familiarity, its meaning and importance, linked with a much larger warehouse space, big enough to accommodate a number of homes—perhaps the twelve of the members at the conference. This appropriateness of place necessarily underpins confidence at the beginning of work in the matrix. To "say goodbye to home" in this dream is an appropriate invocation for every member of this residential conference, linking it to his or her life beyond the conference boundaries, by providing a conduit for that life to enter the conference.

In the home–warehouse image lies also a distinction between domestic, personal objects and warehouse goods in transit. This alludes to a looser sense of ownership of dreams: although personally experienced, they are socially aired and shared, in a space domesticated, made appropriate as a matrix. In the same way that objects in a home reflect the values and the culture of the family, the character of the dreams reflects the culture—the mix of metaphors—in the matrix. A flight of china ducks on a living-room wall may be thought of as equivalent to the group of hedgehogs in the garden of D14:

> D14:   [*This dream started with a phrase, which may be thought of as a linkage to earlier material: "common as muck".*] *Hedgehogs come into a garden in groups. Then something about being in an annex, rather than a house.* [*The matrix was convened in an annex to the main building, which had been a family house.*] *Then someone—the wife of a participant?—encourages me to write all this down.* [*Members had been issued with a notebook in order to record their dreams.*]

Does this dream reflect a sense of the prickliness of participants, and the matrix at that juncture? In displaying objects such as ducks, hedgehogs, and so forth, we inhabit space, personalize it, transform a warehouse or a bare room into living space. Dream images may be seen in part as personalizing and transforming the matrix space by their shared (social) meaning. But in the telling, in the divination, also lies anxiety.

In D1, the dense ring of policemen is threatening. Here are images of law and order and of its confrontation, with civil rights and survival (as in the vivid media images seen during the miners' strike in the United Kingdom during 1990). Uncertainty (and some of the guilt of *The Third Man*?) seems to underlie the sewer escape: the uncertainty about dwelling in the warehouse, about the activity of social dreaming, about the orderliness (and lawfulness) of dreams that drive the dreamer underground to the wild realm of hedgehogs and waste-matter. The sewer was seen as a dream-place in later dreams, a hidden, subconscious territory that carries a waste that fertilizes and enriches and operates in some ways differently from the law and order of above-ground reason.

In leaving the visible warehouse for the hidden sewer, the dreamer suggests how inappropriate a place the everyday seems for dreaming; that rational force, management structures, all the prosaics of daily ritual are ordering yet diminishing us. The escape is one from impotence, a running towards a greater freedom, a journey from light, through darkness to enlightenment, which will be expressed in the final dreams of the conference, as we shall see.

Our first sighting of the Third Man in the film involves a cat ingratiating itself over a pair of immaculate shoes and trouser cuffs; the rest of the figure is mysteriously hidden in shadow. This evokes a dreamlike expression of feelings, rather than clarity from a filmic image. It is compounded by a tantalizing familiarity with the invisible—a familiarity, exclusive for a man now dead, here, visited on one, living. Here is an odd sense of immortality which anticipates many later dream situations that involved scenes with people already dead, who in dream were alive and active. (The dreamer, in D2, described later, evoked such an image.) This is much the same as with one's lost childhood, which is made immortal by memory and by dream!

With growing mystery in *The Third Man* grows an awareness of crime. The setting is 1948, post-war Vienna; battered, bare brick buildings separated by heaps of war-debris, islands of "no-man's-land", despoiling a sense of whole, of normality; a grim reminder of war, the lack of law and order, and the need for social and physical reconstruction.

Here is a setting for a conference, consisting of the arbitrary (disordered) group of people, a motley of unknown (as yet) dreams, a shared sense for reconstruction, of challenges to law and order, of dealing with the invisible, the dead, of power and of anxiety.

Beginning by alluding to anxiety is both frank and appropriate, since to acknowledge it is to allow disturbing and other feelings a rightful place during work. In the beginning was the word, and the word was anxiety. Furthermore, announcing anxiety is a call to work while there is time. Perhaps in response to D1, the first matrix provided the largest number of dreams. In the film and in the dream "the chances of escape seem slim", unless we transform the sewer-hunt into another experience which, at its unavoidable end, is enriching.

Anxiety may have influenced the second part of D1, for jail seems, for the moment, to have been avoided—another person going there instead. In this part, the ordering and management of figures constrained on a page form a motive weaker than either jail—a building ringed by bars—or a building ringed by police, as if through such gradations we may approach anxiety and ordering in the matrix. There is perhaps a shift, too, from an issue about policing and the law to a question of what is the law of dreaming— is it a straightforward form of accountancy, or, as seems implied in the complex imagery, a more difficult lore to understand?

Another significant change is a change from one to two fugitives—"both in the same boat". There is also a link through debt, "he owes me money", a common interest in paying and being paid (perhaps an extension of the process of giving to and taking from each other's dreams?). Is this collusion for survival or growth? Two joined reduce the sense of anxiety and the need for flight. The dream journey becomes manageable when the running stops. Imprisoned by the convention that rings the matrix, some freedoms may be enlarged through the way we relate there. We are all in the same society-boat, the same SDM-boat. Some concerted effort (like paddling, rowing, hoisting a collective sail, "telling and associating to dreams") would enable a journey of some sort for the imprisoned or becalmed.

There were numerous journey-dreams, which involved family, cars, buses, boats, taxis, trains, a lift, roller-skating, eating, nudity, motor-cycle formations, marches, flying, office removals, rambling, and wandering in medieval towns—a rich geographicality, another example of dialogic transformation.

Sewers are inoperative without water, to which, also, boats belong. It was raining during SDM1 and much of the conference. Water was one of the main themes, being evoked as transporter, as food, tears, rain, damp, holy water, mould, and as light at the bottom of a well. It was a variegated vehicle for feelings and motion, for life, for sadness, for death, for visions, for waste, ablutions, and blessings.

Let us return to the kiosk in the earlier part of D1. In the film *The Third Man*, this was a circular, phallic-looking chef's hat plastered with decrepit posters, the otherwise mute and only object in an empty square, inside which was the give-away entry to the city's sewers along which the fugitive escaped. It was a sewer vent that looked like a kiosk, one of those numerous utilitarian objects in cities which we often overlook. But appearances and need dictated it as a kiosk for the dreamer, with filmic associations.

Kiosks, a European city phenomenon, are diminutive warehouses storing and retailing small items, such as papers, cards, matches, and telephone calls. They are, in the phrase that John Summerson coined, miniature shelters, or "aedicular architecture" (Summerson, 1949). An aedicule is a sort of shrine or small niche, often framed by columns and pediment, and housing a statue; or, more loosely, the classical framing marking a window or a door. It has been related to those diminutive play-huts that children make, to which they more easily belong than to spaces in the wider world. Their play is better contained in child-sized spaces—niches appropriate for their fantasies and dreams. The kiosk in *The Third Man* similarly signifies, protects, and contains the sewer entrance.

There is a sense here for the need to signify, protect, and contain the social dreaming: firstly, with the matrix itself aedicularly transformed, containing perhaps transitional objects of childhood whose stable values survive our maturation into the wider world's instabilities; secondly, the voicing of a need to protect and to enshrine something (oneself?) during the act of social dreaming.

This is an example of the making, or re-making, of defining characteristics and boundaries of our world, of an aedicular "systemically linked cosmos" (Lawrence, 1991); as if, by association with an earlier bit of the dream, "ringed" and with attendant anxiety. The broaching of anxiety is significant in at least two ways: firstly, as a true mirror of feelings, as dreams are; secondly, as anxiety about the task and its accomplishment, as a spur to work in the matrix—this, the carrot; the former, the stick.

Anthony Brennan (1986), discussing our understanding of Lear's problems and responses to his "epic saga", says,

> "We can define them and relate to them more effectively in their parallels with and radical contrast to the experience of Gloucester", which is the other story which Shakespeare patched into his play, and which acts as an aedicular story through which we are enabled to reach into the epic. [p. 6]

The same process is apparent in the matrix.

There is a glancing reference to structures in D1. The warehouse, a square shape, the circle (ring) of policemen, the circular kiosk, contrasting with the more complicated and indeterminate spiral layout of chairs in the matrix (representing "the task"?), and the invisible labyrinthine structure of the sewers (the process of social dreaming?). The room layout seems apt for the dialogic processes in the matrix, although there seems to be a wish for simpler structures. However, during the ten SDM sessions, the menacing circle became transformed finally into a fecund well of light and water, for health and farewell: the dreams get disbursed in the light of the well (SDM10, D1). The hidden sewer is replaced by the well, which is open ended, healthily fished-in with open bucket on a snaking rope connected traditionally to an aedicular winding mechanism, Jack and Jill–scaled. If one looks down into a well, one sees one's self and the vast sky beyond, held in a tiny ring of watery light—a paradox appropriate to social dreaming, of looking down into the earth to find oneself and to see the sky (Oeser, 1992)!

This transformation is already evident in the second and third dreams following D1 (SDM1):

D2: *I have a mysterious work placement in a family staying in a modern chalet [reminiscent of the conference centre]. My parents arrive to check out the families, which I much resent. I am young-yet-old. In fact, my mother died a long time ago. Suddenly we become friends. Then out come two endearing dog–sheep; the families pair off by sex.*

D3: *I am in a lecture theatre with banked seats; the SDM cannot start because someone is always leaving.*

Both D1 and D2 involve senses of "home ": a warehouse-home and a modern chalet-home, the latter more familiar. Helping with managing, from the end of D1, evolves in D2: money transforms into people, the commonality of families. A family may be thought of as an aedicular matrix or aedicular community. This is a response to the "run, run" of D1, in that escape may be achieved through dreaming about families. The third dreamer (D3) seems to confirm an emphasis on the matrix by the immediate link with the preceding dream. "Banked seats" might suggest a "stepped-pyramid" seating layout and be a reference to power (that of the Pharaohs) and pyramidal management structures (an association with authority was made at this time); or it might allude to the need for clear sight-lines to the task in the matrix–auditorium (which the conference layout was not), to the wish to see more than dark, wet sewers allow, to come out of the dark and up into the seen, clean world.

In D2, resentment is transformed into friendship, although the outcome is a dog–sheep, a (new) Beast Theme which was to permeate the conference. Another outcome is pairing, by similarity, in this case by sexuality (a theme taken up later). *The Third Man* is thus banished—to be transformed into one of those paradoxical beasts which haunt us? In the film, knowledge about the Third Man is deadly: the Caretaker who saw him is murdered; it is wiser not to meddle, to let sleeping dogs lie. In the end, Harry Lyme turns out to be the Minotaur killed in the labyrinthine sewers.

The dog–sheep is a linguistic pair, the halves interdependent. For without sheep there are no sheep dogs and, without dogs, any dog–sheep. Both are "in the same boat" of D1. Here, perhaps, is an attempt to personify anxiety in an object, concrete beasts being easier to handle than feelings. Yet one is left with an awkward thought—perhaps it is the hidden beast in ourselves, which needs to be joined, un-jailed, and which needs to be interdependently managed!

So, we have seen how, from the start, the characters of the conference and the agenda were heralded with evocative possibilities. How, so early, there was a consensus, if diffuse. How uncannily this is like a play! Now let us turn to one.

The first scene

King Lear opens in mid-conversation, as if the two senior courtiers had stepped in off the street, talking the language of the street, rather than that of the theatre. There is no poetic "if music be the food of love, play on" of *Twelfth Night*; rather, a linguistic extension of the world that was familiar to the audience, a two-way link that develops speedily and transforms familiarity into the epic tempests of the mind, almost beyond cognizance:

> *Kent*: I thought the King had more affected the Duke of Albany than Cornwall.
>
> *Gloucester*: It did always seem to us, but now in the division of the kingdom it appears not which of the Dukes he values most; for qualities are so weighed that curiosity in neither can make choice of either's moiety.
>
> *Kent*: Is not this your son, my lord?
>
> *Gloucester*: His breeding, sir, hath been at my charge. I have so often blushed to acknowledge him that now I am brazed to 't.

> *Kent*:   I cannot conceive you.
>
> *Gloucester*:   Sir, this man's mother could, whereupon she grew roundwombed and had indeed, sir, a son for her cradle ere she had a husband for her bed. Do you smell a fault?

(1.1.1–15)

At once, a weird familiarity and the machinations of families predominate. A sense of "alternatives" grows: of children, the bastard son Edmund opposite Edgar the heir; of the balance of favour for Albany/Goneril or Cornwall/Regan; of Cordelia feeling the odd (third) man out; a balancing of Gloucester's private sensuality and Cordelia's shy love with the pomp of the court and its public, overblown speeches. For instance, following Goneril's speech of love, "Beyond all manner of so much I love you":

> *Regan*:   I am made of that self mettle as my sister,
> And I prize me at her worth. In my true heart
> I find she names my very deed of love—
> Only she comes too short, that I profess
> Myself an enemy to all other joys
> Which the most precious square of sense possesses,
> And find I am alone felicitate
> In your dear highnesses love.

(1.1.69–76)

How true this turns out to be! For Regan, in abetting the putting out of Gloucester's eyes, then exceeds her sister in flattery and cruelty. This flattery is an alternative to the caring bluntness of Kent: "Be Kent unmannerly/When Lear is mad . . . to plainness honour's bound" (1.1.145). Already, what "seems" has more weight than what "is", what ought socially to be said overwhelms personal sincerity. It is the racked exchange between Cordelia and her father that unleashes his rash halving of the kingdom:

> *Lear*:   . . . Now our joy, . . . what can you say to draw
> A third more opulent than your sisters? Speak.
>
> *Cordelia*:   Nothing, my lord.
>
> *Lear*:   Nothing?
>
> *Cordelia*:   Nothing.

Lear: Nothing will come of nothing. Speak again.

Cordelia: Unhappy that I am, I cannot heave
My heart into my mouth.
I love your majesty
According to my bond, no more nor less.

(1.1.82 ff.)

By the end of the play these "nothings" will be transformed into Lear's "Never", five times murmured as he dies, and capped by Edgar's, the only young survivor left at the end, ". . . We that are young/Shall never see so much, nor live so long" (5.3.301).

In the use of language in the first scene are formed the habits of the play. The plain prose and unsettling sense unconfined by line contrast with an intensity produced by the rhymed meter that transforms the language of love and of truth throughout. For example, a true king wooing a "worthless" princess:

France: Fairest Cordelia, that art most rich, being poor; . . .
Not all the dukes of wat'rish Burgundy
Can buy this unprized, precious maid of me.
Bid them farewell, Cordelia, though unkind.
Thou losest here, a better where to find.

(1.1.250 ff.)

Similarly, later, the Fool gently lectures Lear on perspicaciousness:

Have more than thou showest
Speak less than thou knowest . . .

(1.4.117 ff.)

Edgar concludes the play with the rhymes tolling the end of this great epic. This is reminiscent of conference members who turned to the heightened language of poetry in order to express the inexpressible associations to their dreams towards the conference's end.

All the play's ingredients, its "currency" (Lawrence & Daniel, 1982, p. 3), are displayed in the first scene of Lear—not in parentheses, but in the language of action: the appearances of truth or falsehood; love, honour, and duty to family, to realm; the silence of banishment and the silence of love; madness of the powerful and sense of fools; blindness and foresight; separation and unity.

The paradoxes deepen our sense of man's fate as observer/ subject rather than controller of Nature—it is Lear's almost automatic reflex to events, after the division of the kingdom, that transforms him from an imperious king into a kneeling father:

> *Lear*:   Let it be so. Thy truth then be thy dower;
> For by the sacred radiance of the sun,
> The mysteries of Hecate, and the night,
> By all the operation of the orbs
> From whom we do exist and cease to be,
> Here I disclaim all my paternal care,
> Propinquity, and property of blood,
> And as a stranger to my heart and me
> Hold thee from this forever.
> The barbarous Scythian,
> Or he that makes his generation messes
> To gorge his appetite, shall to my bosom
> Be as well neighboured, pitied and relieved
> As thou, my sometime daughter.
>
> (1.1.108–119)

> *Lear*:   . . . Come, [Cordelia] let's away to prison.
> We two alone will sing like birds i'th'cage.
> When thou cost ask me blessing, I'll kneel down
> And ask of thee forgiveness; so we'll live,
> And pray and sing . . .
>
> (5.3.8ff.)

This perplexingly complex world—not only outside, but also the inner tempest of feelings—suffuses the play, from its opening scene.

In this review of the "currency" of the matrix and the play (the money matters in the second part of D1!), I have tried to show how prophetic are the starts of both the conference and the play. What I wish to stress is the process of preparations that the two seem to share, not literary qualities. I suggest that the intuition of the dreamer in the matrix has a similar source to the creative well dipped into by Shakespeare. Everyone has, to some extent, a sense of detail plus a sense of overall form, from "knowing" about life, from being alive (after all, we call ourselves human beings). "There is no alibi for being" (Mikhail Bakhtin).

Foreknowledge

Shakespeare probably knew the form that his play would take (it was composed from two existing stories); he too, would have had an inkling of much of its detail as he started. This accounts for the review of "currency" in the first scene, which we have been looking at.

There was no equivalent agenda for the matrix. No one—including the first dreamer—had any idea of the form and content that the conference would evolve.

The origin of the aptness of the first dream probably lies in the processes of social dreaming, which facilitate the use of almost overlooked information and skills (foreknowledge) that all of us have gleaned from our experience in families and later in the outside world. This might be defined in longer words as the dynamics of relatedness and knowledge of a shared culture—which was certainly the case of this Birmingham conference, where everyone was from a Western European milieu and the conference language was English. I am uncomfortable with descriptions using "unconscious" since it seems that our skills in using the foreknowledge are conscious, if undervalued (part of our packaged perceptions). Their use probably depends more on the right than the left hemisphere of the brain, with intuitive rather than rational control. It was a conscious decision to tell the first dream, to tell all the dreams, and to associate to them (even knowing that much of the material had unconscious manifestations).

The word "collective" seems a description—but at a distance from the process itself, too abstract. The feet of a crowd may be described as collective: everyone has a pair. But it is in the sharing of a common goal that the individuals—who make up the crowd—will take concerted action and, for instance, march down the Avenue (as if with one pair of feet!). Collective action is the result of many individual decisions (or dreams) whose significance should not be obscured. We should not distance ourselves from such potential working-processes.

I would suggest that this foreknowledge is a resource that may be shared, and that the processes in the matrix help us tap into it. The proposition of D1 is that we can manage our "currency", even if some of us are in jail, as life often appears to be; that better management (possibly more freedom?) seems to arise out of sharing; that (since flight prevents work) the process of flight may be allayed through sharing.

To deal with the suspicion that this was purely a fortuitous start, let us look briefly at the first dream of another session to see whether it has a role similar to the first dream: SDM5, a plateau of expression and sharing, "seemed to make-up a single dream, despite the extraordinary variety of material, . . . a unity of separate and distinct parts" (Oeser, 1992, p. 240).

> D1:   In the 1920s, well-dressed men and women descending from a train in Switzerland greet each other with, "Where were you last night?"

The next two dreams made conscious links with this opening:

> D2:   We were similarly dressed in my dream. It was misty, early morning. We had rifles and were ready to bury things.

> D3:   I also had a travel dream: I was at home with family and friends getting ready to go out. My son came in with many friends. We had a row because the old Volvo couldn't fit everyone in; we needed a hire-car. [The Volvo belonged to earlier times with the kids.] We decided to walk. It was a pleasant walk to "The Bridge", where, magically, a bus was waiting that we took in turns to drive to the restaurant, where we had a good meal.

The laughter that greeted the telling of D1 acknowledged its aptness here—"Last night I was in bed, hopefully dreaming!" each of us felt. The well-dressed people were ourselves (you had to be well-heeled to attend the conference, and to travel in Switzerland); we were dressed to travel—to work, to "be"—in the matrix. By this time, there was a sense of orderly working in SDM5. There was a feeling of orderliness on the social dreaming "plateau", akin to associations with Switzerland of order, of clocks and timetables. There was, perhaps, also a need to acknowledge order and ordering as necessary in trying to manage the rich fare of dreams, which produces anxiety (as we have seen) as well as involvement.

The subjects of anxiety, of sharing, of ordering (managing), and flight (travel can be flight) recur here, as does the transformation of the "run, run" of D1, SDM1, to its end, at the start of this fifth session: in this case, the journey is over, people are alighting from a stationary train, no more clickity-clack, no more tunnels. They have arrived at their destination, for sightseeing or work, or home-coming.

The apt question, "Where were you last night?", is duly answered, and most of the themes developed in the matrix are touched on once again. I feel that this demonstrates that there is a conscious sense of "start", not only for each of the individual matrices, but also for the conference as a whole.

It could be argued that this is scene-setting that participants are dictated to from the start. But this is only one small aspect of the influences on the process of social dreaming, for generated from their commonality members shaped the utterances from the out-set, just as Bakhtin's dialogic model represents readers shaping the utterance as it is taking place, where context may be seen as funda-mental to all human activity. Furthermore, it must be pointed out that all dreams were privately experienced beforehand. The open-ing dreams were chosen, recognized, and felt as apt beginnings; all dreams were chosen and recognized and felt as timely statements, in ways in which a playwright works with his material. We experi-ence a play in our life-terms: it has relevance or meaning because the playwright and we have made these connections. What hap-pens of significance on-stage has first been "lived" off it. Lear (Shakespeare!) bitterly makes the connection; he eventually calls the world "this great stage of fools", which is crowded and action-filled (4.5.179).

Finally

This chapter has illustrated processes of transformation, dem-onstrated something of the systemic linkage, and investigated some of the qualities of language in the social dreaming matrix. These are key concerns in Lawrence's 1991 paper, in which he also alludes to our developing a more integrated, generous, and less destructive future.

The *Tragedy of King Lear* ends with Edgar reflecting,

> The weight of this sad time we must obey,
> Speak what we feel, not what we ought to say.

Dreams can illuminate "what we feel", can often inspire what we ought to feel. The SDM seems to allow us to resist the law and order of "ought", as well as to allow a creative working-out with dialogic transformations of a perplexingly complex mass of individually experienced life-situations into something more deeply shared than is usual. The process uses a greater range of our knowledge and skills than usual. I left the conference with a renewed vision of a wholer world, and a new conviction about ways in which to begin—new ways to stand on our own feet, with a richer sense of dependence. Lest footless angels fear to tread, let *Lear's* Fool, looking into the heart of mankind, have the last word:

> . . . I'll speak a prophecy ere I go:
> When priests are more in word than matter;
> When brewers mar their malt with water;
> When nobles are their tailors' tutors;
> No heretics burned, but wenches suitors,
> Then shall the realm of Albion
> Come to great confusion.
>
> When every case in law is right;
> No squire in debt nor no poor knight;
> When slanderers do not live in tongues,
> Nor cutpurses come not to throngs;
> When usurers tell their gold i' th' field,
> And bawds and whores do churches build,
> Then comes the time, who lives to see't,
> That going shall be used with feet.
> This prophecy Merlin shall make; for I live before his
> time.

(3.2.79 ff.)

CHAPTER SEVEN

Thinking aloud:
contributions to three dialogues

David Armstrong

A context for dialogue

In 1989, Gordon Lawrence invited Bruce Reed and me to work with him as consultants on a new and highly original venture. For some time, Lawrence had been preoccupied with the idea of "social dreaming"—that is, with the possibility that dreaming might have a social dimension, which, if it could be appropriately framed, might become a new and powerful means for exploring and understanding human relatedness in its social and cultural aspects. He has vividly described the mixture of experience, intuition, and luck that set him off on this journey (Lawrence, 1991). By the time he came to talk to us, he had already designed and mounted a number of programmes, in collaboration with professional colleagues, in Israel, Germany, and Sweden, which put the idea to work. He was interested in doing something in this country and wondered whether The Grubb Institute would be willing to co-sponsor such a programme here.

It did not take long to grasp that Lawrence was on the track of something very exciting, which both linked to and also extended the Institute's recent involvement in "explorations in social consciousness". Some six months later, the first social dreaming programme in the United Kingdom took place, over five days, at Wast Hills House, Birmingham. There were some two dozen members, women and men, mainly British but with a strong contingent from the Republic of Ireland, as well as an Australian and a Swede. They included organizational consultants, psychotherapists, social workers, educationalists, writers, and religious. Most were familiar with experiential approaches to understanding group processes—sufficiently familiar to be able to differentiate this programme from the more standard "group relations" conference or event.

The programme was repeated the following year and again in 1991, sponsored on this occasion by IMAGO East-West, a recently founded Institute for Intercultural Psychodynamic Research, based in London. I participated in all three of these programmes, from which the "contributions to dialogues" presented here are taken.

"Dialogues" was the name given to the second of three main events that made up each programme. The first and core event was called the "Social Dreaming Matrix". In this, participants and consultants met for an hour and a half at the beginning and end of each day, before breakfast and after dinner. The aim was described as "To help participants make creative use of their dream experiences to discover their unconscious political and spiritual awareness of their social world". The primary task, or operating process, was stated as "To associate to and interpret the latent social meanings of dreams available in the matrix".

The third event, at first referred to as "Mutual Consultation Sets" and subsequently "Systemic Consultation Sets", provided a setting in which participants presented experiences from their current work in or with organizations, which other participants then explored through offering working hypotheses which could be tested by questions put to and answered by the presenter, through the mediating role of a designated "chair".

The "Dialogues" took place each day in a large room with chairs placed in lines so that members directly faced each other. All participants and consultants took part, and the only difference in role was that one member, usually a consultant, started the dialogue, on a theme of his or her choice.

The intention was that the dialogues should be an opportunity to present reflections arising from one's own professional interests and concerns which directly or indirectly related to the domain of enquiry that the programme was addressing. This could be crudely described as the use of systemic and psychoanalytic thinking to enlarge and explore the meaning of experiences in a social and cultural milieu.

There was another, perhaps more important, intention. Dialogue implies parity, exchange. At the same time, these social dreaming programmes were a deliberate attempt to break into new ground; this was as true for the consultants as for the participants. We were encouraged and encouraged ourselves to work in the dialogues from those areas of thinking that could be described as emergent, at least for us—to think aloud in the presence of others. So the primary task of the event offered to participants was simply "To be available for thought". Correspondingly, in preparing to open a dialogue—even where some particular topic or title had already been chosen—one needed to try to approach this afresh, without assuming that one knew exactly what needed to be said, but, on the other hand, without burdening or seducing participants by apologizing for one's own uncertainty.

Lawrence suggested a number of rules of thumb: state what was in one's mind in propositions, or "working hypotheses"; restrict what one said to 20 minutes at the outside; avoid getting drawn into answering questions or engaging in debate—ideally, to say nothing further. In other words, opening a dialogue was providing opportunities for dialogue to others, not seeking to draw others into dialogue with oneself.

It was not always easy to observe these rules, but the gains of doing so were very marked. By letting go, as it were, of what one had formulated, it became possible to approach it or see it differently, as an occasion for linking.

This was the context in and for which the following scripts were written. In each case, they were sketched out the night before, more or less as delivered next day. Although I had a rough idea of what I wanted to say, in writing things down they sometimes developed in a different direction to the one I had expected. They are transcribed here as spoken at the time, with minimal corrections and additions.

I am not sure whether they add up to a consistent chain of thought. In so far as they do, it will be apparent how much they are influenced by the work of Wilfred Bion, even if, as is likely, they distort it.

Finding thoughts

I want to state three working hypotheses, the first two of which can be treated as propositions:

I   *There are two kinds of thinking, which for convenience can be labelled Thinking 1 and Thinking 2*

- In Thinking 1
    — thought or thoughts are the product of thinking; they evolve out of thinking

    — thought or thoughts require a thinker; they owe their existence to a thinker

    (These two characteristics can be summed up philosophically as the proposition that thinking is epistemologically and existentially prior to thought.)

    — such thoughts are capable of being owned; they are like pieces of personal property—"my thoughts", "your thoughts", "our thoughts"

    — they are things that we use and do things with; we elaborate them, manipulate them, spell them out, relate them to other thoughts—our own or other people's

    — they can be either true or false

    — they require exegesis; someone who has skills to explain and justify or demonstrate them

    — they are capable of being taught; things one has to learn to be able to think for oneself

    — they are things that we control; we own and so can disown them, develop them as we will

- In Thinking 2
    - thought or thoughts are not the product of thinking; rather, thinking is an apparatus that evolves for the communication of thoughts
    - thought or thoughts do not require that a thinker exists and do not owe their existence to a thinker, although a thinker is needed to "receive" them and to "publish" them, just as a wireless receiver picks up and publishes radio waves

    (These two characteristics can be summed up philosophically as the proposition that thought or thoughts are epistemologically and existentially prior to thinking.)

    - such thoughts are not objects of ownership, they are no one's personal property—not mine, not yours, not ours
    - they are neither true nor false; they just are; they have being
    - they do not require exegesis, but the practice of awareness

    (They may require finding adequate words to express them or "contain" them, but skill with words or other symbolic operations cannot substitute for the primary act of awareness. They are not demonstrated, explained, and justified but are voiced through the experience of making them public—to oneself, to another, or to others.)

    - they are not capable of being taught, but are capable of being shown; they are not things one learns about, but things one learns of and from
    - we do not control them or develop them; rather, they control and develop us

The concept of thought or thoughts in Thinking 2 requires some additional specification. If thoughts are "entities" that are independent of a thinker, what kind of entities are they? A tentative answer is:

— they are objects of emotional experience, which make their presence felt initially in the sense of something absent, not there: a no-thought

— thought, in Thinking 2, emerges out of something not known, which is felt as a frustration, a limitation, an oppression, a terror, or a mystery

— when this not-known begins to take a shape that can be formulated, it is as if I were being introduced to or "spoken to" myself, or as if we were being introduced to or "spoken to" ourselves

— this introduction or being spoken to oneself or to ourselves is not to oneself or to ourselves alone, but to oneself or ourselves in relatedness to something else: a person, a group, an organization, a society, a world or worlds

(Which is to say, generically, that a thought in Thinking 2 is always located systemically. And this relates to the fact that the object of experience is always contextual, never "private". There is always an implicit presence of the other, internally and/or externally. [In this sense, Wittgenstein's argument against the possibility of a private language expresses, I think, a profound psychological truth.])

II   *The kind of thinking that serves transformations—either in and of the individual or in and of the group—is Thinking 2*

I distinguish between transformation and change, where "change" is something experienced as brought about from without, rather than something released from within. In contrast to transformation, change in this sense is served by Thinking 1.

How do I know the difference between Transformation ↔ Thinking 2 and Change ↔ Thinking 1?

I am not sure that I always do know or can recognize this difference. But I think I can describe what it feels like to be in the presence of Thinking 1 and Thinking 2, through the experience of the encounter between consultant and client. (The following contrast is sharper than is usually the case in reality, where the differences I want to draw attention to are rarely as clear-cut.)

Client 1 comes to you from his or her organization, apparently knowing exactly what the problem is or what he or she expects you to do about it, which often involves doing something with, to, or for somebody else. You are in a situation that can be construed as X, the client, wanting Y, the consultant, to take on a job that X either does not wish to take on personally, or feels unequipped for, or for various reasons would prefer someone else from outside to tackle: as an "expert". Such a client is wishing to exploit the consultant's capacity for Thinking 1—his or her technical, analytic competence, training, and skill. The client is looking for some good Thinking 1 from you and will probably not welcome being offered Thinking 2. He or she may look to you to confirm and give a stamp of approval to something that he or she already knows but cannot convince others of, or to offer useful techniques for achieving something that he or she wants to achieve but is not sure exactly how.

Client 2 comes and appears quite uncertain as to what the problem is. He or she may tell a story that leaves you feeling as uncertain and chaotic too. The client is experiencing a sense of frustration, of the loss of signposts, of turbulence within and without; he or she shares in this experience—that is, it is located inside as well as outside. Such a client is implicitly announcing that he or she is in the ambit of Thinking 2, of an awareness of something waiting to be found and formulated in the act of exploration and interpretation between you.

The sign of this for the consultant, as often as not, is the personal experience of a resistance in the form of impatience, a wish to leap ahead, scan his or her conceptual, analytic skills to offer premature "solutions" or "insights", rather than live with his or her doubts, obscurities, and fears until a pattern emerges that can be given a name, whose meaning can then become available for exploration.

III *My third working hypothesis is difficult to state precisely and is, in fact, a kind of paradox.* One might imagine that thoughts in Thinking 1, depending as they do on individuals' acts of thinking, were ephemeral, whereas thoughts in Thinking 2, which by definition pre-exist the individual thinker, were more enduring.

Yet my experience suggests that the reality is the other way round. The thoughts produced in Thinking 1 often last an awfully long time, sometimes to our cost. Institutions are created to transmit them. The thoughts evolved or received out of Thinking 2, once they have found a good-enough expression, tend to become unimportant. Instead, they lead to the finding of other thoughts, to new thoughts that replace them. (This can be compared with the way in which creative artists, while they remain creative, are often not much interested in their previous work.)

This seems to be because, once a found thought has been adequately expressed, it leads to the changing or mutating of the reality of which it was a formulation. As it mutates, it then becomes something else, so that the past thought passes away. This is why I believe that it is not right to say that thoughts in Thinking 2 are "true" or "false". In describing Thinking 1 and Thinking 2 earlier, I referred to thoughts in Thinking 2 as things that "just are", that "have being". Perhaps it would be better to say that they are things that are found to "promote development" and in the process, so to speak, do themselves out of a job.

So, paradoxically, the appropriate philosophical model for Thinking 2 seems not to be Plato's idea of eternal forms but rather Trotsky's idea of permanent revolution—which is why Thinking 2 is always a bit terrifying.

Change and transformation

1. *There is a distinction in kind between change and transformation*

Both change and transformation yield or convey information: a difference that makes a difference (McCulloch, 1965).

In the case of change, the difference that makes a difference is seen or experienced from outside: a change of circumstance, a change in the environment, new market conditions, new legislation, new technological inventions, new regimes, trends, lifestyles, new partners in our private and public lives. These changes may be experienced as a threat, a challenge, an imposition, an opportunity, a hope. One way or another, we have to come to terms with them. Consciously or unconsciously, coming to terms with them is likely to involve a mixture of seeking to maximize anticipated gains and minimize feared losses. There is also always a shadow side of change: inertia—the tendency of all living systems to seek to remain the same, preserve what is.

In the case of transformation, the difference that makes a difference is seen or experienced not from outside but from inside. Something happens inside us or inside our system: family, organization, society, nation. Unlike change, this something happening may not present itself as a locatable difference, but rather as an uneasy awareness of something that is not the same, which often carries an aura of threat to the individual's or organization's sense of identity.

This threat, however, comes from within, not without—though we may seek to project it outwards, to turn it into change, as it were. (There is such a thing as "flight to change".) The difference that makes a difference in transformation is at first a not-known; its meaning or significance has to be discovered. We need not so much to come to terms with it as, by allowing it the space to evolve, let it enable us to come to terms with ourselves. In the face of change, the individual or the organization discovers what it wants or does not want. In the face of transformation, it discovers what it is, or is becoming. Just as there is a shadow side of change—inertia—so also there is a shadow side of transformation—resistance, fundamentally resistance to development.

2   *Management of change and management of transformation involve differences of focus and response*

Management of change requires action and/or reaction depending on whether the change is welcomed or not welcomed. It involves the exercise of power and the mobilization of fight.

Management of transformation requires not action and reaction but (to borrow a good title) "attention and interpretation"

(Bion, 1970). It involves the exercise of authority, in the sense of a speaking out, in role, of my experience and the mobilization of insight.

Management of change focuses on manifest or explicit intentions and aims. Management of transformation focuses on latent or implicit meanings.

The terms I have used to refer to management of transformation invite questions: attention to what, interpretation of what, meanings of or in what?

3   *I suggest that the answer to all these questions is the same: the object of attention, interpretation, and the disclosure of meaning is, invariably, emotional experience*

It is the readiness and capacity to entertain emotional experience which serves and elicits transformations.

This statement provokes a further question: what is "emotional experience"—or, more specifically, what is the emotional experience that serves and elicits transformations? I want to say two things about this, one to do with time and the other with space.

We often tend to think of emotional experience as something present, compounded of sensation, feeling, and associated imagery or ideas. This something present may, of course, relate to the past—the emotions aroused in us by recollection—or to the future—the emotions aroused in us by anticipation, when we imagine a future event as already here. In all of these cases, the experience appears to us as more or less definite and nameable: this is what I am feeling now.

It can be argued, however, that primary emotional experience is not at all like this. It predates any ability to differentiate and hence to name. What we ordinarily think of as emotional experience is something learnt, communicable, and public. I want to emphasize, rather, what is not learned, not communicable in the ordinary ways involving language and abstraction, but is most certainly communicable in extra-ordinary ways. These extra-ordinary ways involve a kind of mental "passaging" from one to another or other, a lodging in or infection of an individual or a group (in psychoanalytic terms, projective identification).

Primary emotional experience in this sense often has a premonitory quality. It is like so-called signal anxiety in that it represents an as yet unfocused awareness of an emotional state not yet fully present, which, as Bion put it, "casts its shadow before". I suggest that it is the capacity to entertain this anticipatory awareness of things not the same—without recourse to evasion, denial, or lying in the service of a reality that is about to become an illusion—that opens the individual or the group, organization, society to the possibility of transformation: to learning from experience, rather than simply learning by experience. I suggest that this capacity is closely linked to the capacity to dream and to the significance of the dream in mental life, which W. B. Yeats paradoxically described as the "beginning of responsibility". Dreams, if we treat them seriously, prefigure transformations. They provide the evidence for and give some symbolic formulation to the emotional experience in the air.

Lastly, I offer a comment on the space of emotional experience. Here, also, I think that our common usage and ways of thinking can be misleading and perhaps defensive. Ordinarily, we tend to locate emotional experience in the individual, as if such experiences were matters of private ownership. How often in group relations conferences has one heard someone say "That's what *I* feel" or "That's not what *I* feel—speak for yourself". One understands the irritation with the use of "we". I am often nonetheless surprised at our readiness not to be equally irritated by the use of "I"—as if one could be so sure not just of what one is feeling, but also of the extent of one's participation or non-participation in the feelings of others. I suggest that emotional experience is very rarely located within a purely individual space. Psychoanalysis, for example, is not the investigation of the emotional experience of the individual alone. It is the investigation of the emotional experience of the pair. But if you extend your attention outwards, is it simply the investigation of the emotional experience of the pair? Is it not also the investigation of the relatedness of the pair to the emotional experience of the group or the society?

We do not know just where the boundaries of emotional experience should be drawn. My suggestion is that emotional experience is co-extensive with the system-in-mind. If one can tune into this experience as a systemic property, one can begin to get a purchase on the systemic reality that is in the process of beginning to be. This reality is the ground of transformation, because the paradox of transformation is that discovering what is real—if an individual, group, or organization can live long enough with the pain—liberates the energy to evolve something new. Finding leads to making.

Questioning boundaries

In the work that I do with groups and organizations, I am constantly focusing on and preoccupied with boundaries. By now I almost instinctively think of a system as simply, in Gregory Bateson's phrase, "activities with a boundary" (Bateson, 1973). This preoccupation with boundaries in organizational settings involves trying to understand in my encounter with a client—that is, in the emotional experience between the client and myself—the relation of inside and outside, part and whole, reality and fantasy, work and non-work, within a continually shifting, external context.

When I work with an individual manager or group of managers reflecting on their working experience, I am always seeking to discern the patterning of their relatedness to the organization (or, more precisely, to the "organization-in-the-mind"). [In using the phrase "organization-in-the-mind", I intend this to be taken literally and not just metaphorically. That is, I take the view that if one is working with a client to understand his or her working experience in an institutional setting, one is never working with the "individual" alone but with the organization-in-the-individual, as part of the emotional experience presented.] This involves trying to discern the relatedness of the person in role to the system and the way that behaviour is being shaped in relation to implicit and explicit constructions of what is fitting, apt, constructive, creative, or simply expected within boundaries of territory, task, technique, and time.

For me, it is natural to think of management or management-of-self-in-role as a boundary function: a way of scrutinizing, analysing, and guiding one's behaviour (one's activities, decisions, and plans) in relation to some conception, always subject to revision, of the boundary on which one stands by virtue of one's position within some system or sub-system, and the transactions taking place across that boundary (Lawrence, 1979).

As I see it, a "boundary" represents a mental act of differentiation or separation between two interacting spaces or surfaces:

- inside and outside
- this and not this
- I and not I
- we and not we

Every boundary implies acts of exclusion and acts of inclusion, of taking in and putting out. These acts of exclusion and inclusion, taking in and putting out, are intrinsic to all development, growth, work, thought.

In recent years, however—and perhaps this is related to becoming older, or older in a certain way, with a certain style, a certain resistance—I have found myself increasingly questioning the significance of boundaries both in myself, in my clients, and in my experiences of institutional, social, and political life.

This process of questioning boundaries was powerfully stimulated, some three years ago, when I read a book called *All My Sins Remembered and The Other Side of Genius* (Bion, 1985). This consists of a series of letters written by Wilfred Bion to his wife and family over a period of thirty years. It was through Bion's work that I first became interested in group processes, and I have retained ever since a fascination not only with the content of his thinking, and about the experience and practice of analytic insight in individuals and groups, but also with his way of thought, his refusal to be idolized, contained, expounded, rendered harmless through discipleship.

Anyone at all familiar with group relations conferences will have experience of how very precisely in such events the staff work to maintain boundaries: of time, territory, task, modes of relation to members inside and outside sessions, according to their conception of the apt, appropriate staff role. I have to say that I share this culture, this way of working, which Pierre Turquet once referred to as the "culture of primary task implementation". But—

and there is a but—there are times when one wonders not so much when this culture is under explicit attack, but more when it seems to be functioning only too well.

The letter that caught my attention was written by Bion to his wife during one such conference in America, in which he had agreed to take part after many years' absence from group work as an ordinary member of staff. He describes how he was sitting in the opening plenary and found himself engaged in a conversation with one of the members. Suddenly, in a body, the staff rose and left the room. He was left there as it were in mid-sentence, a bit nonplussed, but after a moment or two he disengaged and went up to his bedroom. After a few minutes sitting in his room, there was knock on the door. Ken Rice, one of the conference staff, and the man above all others who had evolved the group relations method in a conference setting, following Bion's model of group work, entered the room. He said that the staff were very worried because they had gone to their workroom for a post-plenary meeting and had expected Bion to be there. Bion got up and left with Rice to rejoin them. But to his wife he adds this wry comment:

"I had not realized that Ken Rice's theory of groups depended on split-second timing."

I found myself roaring with laughter, which I think was also the laughter of release, the release born from a certain inspired mischievousness.

For some time, I played around with this experience inside me. It contributed to things that I was beginning to write, but without forming into anything very definite, except an experience of finding that I was taking more risks in the work that I was doing.

Then, earlier this year, I attended a special conference arranged at the University of Kent on Bion's work. There was one lovely paper, presented by a young woman post-graduate student, Nicola Worledge, on Bion's concept of the "Language of Achievement". In the course of her paper, she referred to an image used by Bion (I think in one of his Brazilian discussions with psychoanalysts), when he spoke of a sculpture as "capturing light". She went on to say this:

"The form of a work of art captures meaning which lies outside of its boundaries."

I could not get her phrase out of my mind. It sounded inside me like a ground base to an endless set of variations.

Might not this statement also be true of the dream, or of the collective dreams recorded as myths? Might it not be true of the process of naming, or indeed of any formulated thought? It seemed to imply or promise an extraordinary openness within a bounded space. It suggested a way of looking at any boundary in a new way, not just as container *of* meaning but as a container *for* meaning: never determinate, always unfolding, continually being found and made (to borrow a formulation of Donald Winnicott's).

I want to resist the temptation to use this thought as the basis for a new act of exclusion and division.

The working hypothesis I offer for exploration is simply this:

- *Every bounded entity—the self and its products; human artifacts; the social artifacts that are groups, institutions, societies, nations—can be simultaneously seen as a container* of *meaning and a container* for *meaning.*

If one thinks, say, of the dream as a container *of* meaning, as I think Freud did, one looks for the interpretation, as though the dream were a kind of disguised invention, to be probed through the tools of association and interpretation for its hidden but certain meaning, which is there waiting to be found—multi-layered, but in principle *knowable*.

If one thinks of the dream as a container *for* meaning, as I think some later analysts have implicitly done, one thinks of it as a structure, inchoate and opaque, that captures meanings that lie not simply within but outside its boundaries: something indeterminate, whose meanings may proliferate and change, a point of evolution rather than a product for resolution, something found and made, lost, found, and made again in a new formulation.

Translate this into social or institutional terms: one can think of, say, a school as a container *of* meaning. To think in this way is to think of a school in terms of its explicit and implicit intentionality—the aim or task it sets out to frame, and the way that structures and resources are deployed in service of this aim and frame the interactions between children as pupils and adults as teachers. Simultaneously, it is to think of a school in terms of its established culture—its particular way of doing things, its characteristic defences, its particular traditions and rituals, spoken and unspoken—and the tension between this culture and the school's intentionality. The school as a container of meaning is viewed as determinate; that is, there is an anticipated answer to the questions, what is this school for and what is this school actually doing? The management of a school, seen as a container of meaning, is about working with the tension between intentionality and reality, reviewing each in the light of the other. Intentionality and reality are both seen as different facets, different aspects of the life of the school, of what happens within it. The aim of management is to bring the two into a reasonable concordance.

To think of a school as a container *for* meaning, on the other hand, is to hold the boundary of the school in mind as something that is always open to question. It is to provide a mental space in which it is possible to ask: what is the meaning of "school" or of "this school" now, what is it that is evolving unconsciously in the interactions that this boundary frames in this society? It is to treat school, as I think one can treat any name, as an emergent property, which both identifies but is also always waiting to be born, which contains—if I can now borrow two telling phrases from Bion's late psychoanalytic novel (1991)—both "the past presented" and "the shadow of the future cast before".

As with institutions—hospitals, prisons, businesses, churches, psychoanalysis, group relations conferences—so too with societies or nations. "What is England now?" How can one frame such a question in a meaningful way?

I offer two suggestions: by going beyond survival—that is, by letting the question of survival go in one's mind—and by maintaining what I once heard a child psychotherapist describe, in a marvellously simple phrase, as a state of "alert passivity" (not, alas, a notable characteristic of managers and leaders).

Neither suggestion is without risk. Letting survival go risks annihilation, death. For most of us, alert passivity is not tolerable for very long, and, of course, one can never know for sure what the outcome will be.

However, if one is concerned with the management of transformation, as contrasted with the management simply of change, whether one is a consultant or a practitioner, I think that this deep end may always have to be jumped into, sooner or later.

CHAPTER EIGHT

Creating new cultures:
the contribution of social dreaming

Thomas A. Michael

C reating a new corporate culture has become a popular topic for chief executives and for consultants in the United States. In my home city of Philadelphia, Pennsylvania, the giant pharmaceutical corporation, Smith, Kline & Beecham underwent a significant reorganization, accompanied by plant closings and large-scale layoffs, in 1987. Chief Executive Officer (CEO) Henry A. Wendt was quoted as explaining these dramatic moves by saying, "We need to change our corporate culture". Such a statement would likely not have been made five years earlier, before the publication in 1982 of the business best seller, *Corporate Cultures: The Rites and Rituals of Corporate Life*, by two consultants, Terrence Deal and Allen Kennedy.

In view of the faddism that attends business consulting, a sceptic might be forgiven for suspecting that "changing the corporate culture" was just the latest management ploy to justify layoffs in the face of declining profits. Advocates of improving corporate culture intend something much more positive. Deal and Kennedy are followers of Thomas Peters, the advocate of the search for excellence (Peters & Waterman, 1982). The implication is that those in a position to do so may consciously set out to make changes (for the better) in the culture of the group, organization, or society.

Another, and perhaps more significant, movement advocating change in the workplace is Total Quality Management (TQM), as espoused by the followers of W. Edwards Deming. He advocates a complete transformation of management by the application of a system of "profound knowledge". The organization should concentrate on quality, which is simply meeting or exceeding customer expectation. It should eschew mass inspection at the end of the work in favour of improving the process of work along the way. This will do away with competition in favour of cooperation and the elimination of bonuses and merit pay and will drive out fear from the workplace (Deming, 1993). TQM has certainly taken centre stage in the United States. A recent survey by the Delta Consulting Group reported that ninety-eight per cent of CEOs in American corporations disagreed with the statement that TQM is a fad. Ninety-one per cent believe that changing human behaviour is more important than technical improvements, because the biggest challenge is to change the culture of the organization (reported in *USA Today*, 26 July 1993).

The purpose of this chapter is to examine what it means to try to change a culture, to identify some of the difficulties involved in such an enterprise, and to propose a hypothesis about how social dreaming may contribute.

What are we talking about when we speak of culture, or corporate culture? Edgar Schein, one of the pioneers in organizational development, has given a comprehensive statement that culture is:

> ... a pattern of basic assumptions—invented, discovered, or developed by a given group as it learns to cope with its problems of external adaptation and internal integration—that has worked well enough to be considered valid, and, therefore, to be taught to new members as a correct way to perceive, think, and feel in relation to those problems. [Schein, 1985, p. 9]

Trice and Beyer (1993, p. 2) assert that "cultures are collective phenomena that embody people's responses to the uncertainties and chaos that are inevitable in human experiences". They identify six characteristics of cultures as being collective, emotionally charged, historically based, inherently symbolic, dynamic, and inherently fuzzy. It should be emphasized that a characteristic of a culture is that it is powerful and enduring.

Both of these definitions can be applied to civilizations, countries, ethnic groups, occupations, professions, occupational communities, organizations, and groups (Schein, 1985, p. 8).

While definitions of such breadth make it possible to apply the concept of culture to a corporation, at the same time they leave the door open to analytical and practical difficulties. For example, if there are several distinct groups within a single corporation or occupational community, then there may be several cultures residing within it. Which culture is to be changed? What if it is embedded within a larger culture? Is that larger culture then the environment of the embedded culture? What if that larger culture is undergoing change? For example, what do we make of the challenge at the recent international AIDS conference in Vienna for a worldwide cultural change in the treatment of women to ensure them their basic human right to life? How would that influence corporations as well as national cultures?

It was in the 1950s that the field of organization development identified its mission as being intervention in the culture of organizations. Douglas McGregor and Herbert Shephard in the United States and the researchers at the Tavistock Institute in Great Britain had been influenced by Kurt Lewin, the social psychologist, W. R. Bion, the psychoanalyst, and Lloyd Warner, the anthropologist, to apply action research, psychodynamic insights, and social analysis to the workplace. In 1951, Elliot Jaques published a report of consultation with the Glacier Metal Works which included "culture" in its title, *The Changing Culture of a Factory*. These consultants attempted to improve organizational functioning by promoting greater democracy, improved communication, greater productivity, and deeper employee commitment and involvement.

The publication of Peters and Waterman's *In Search of Excellence* (1982) created a much more widespread interest in the examination of how improving the culture of a whole organization could improve climate and productivity. While Schein had previously emphasized process consulting, in his more recent work he has asserted that the consultant should give more attention to the content of what is learned—which is the culture of the organization—than the process (1985, p.44). Moreover, he suggests that greater emphasis be placed on the relationship between culture and leadership, since "the only thing of real importance that leaders can do is create and manage culture" (p. 2).

Davis (1984) approaches his study of organizational culture by distinguishing between fundamental guiding beliefs and daily culture and proposes to study whether there is incongruence between them. W. G. Dyer (1985) has developed a model for understanding the cycle of cultural evolution in organizations. Kets de Vries (Kets de Vries & Miller, 1984) and Allen and Kraft (1982) concentrate on the irrationality or unconscious of the organization.

A most exciting approach to changing organizations is by the use of search conferences, a process devised by Fred and Merrelyn Emery and the late Eric Trist. Marvin Weisbord is an enthusiastic sponsor of the use of search conferences in the United States, having published two books on the topic. Search conferences involve getting not only representatives of the organization or system into the room, but also representatives of all stakeholder groups to join in the activity to "create the corporate future", to use Ackoff's (1981) term. Weisbord (1987) has proposed a "learning curve" for organizational consultancy and management as a new practice theory (p. 261). In it, he summarizes the developments that have taken place in organizational development so far:

> In 1900 Taylor had experts solve problems for people—scientific management. In 1950 Lewin's descendants started everybody solving their own problems—participative management. About 1965 experts discovered systems thinking and began improving whole systems, for other people. Now we are learning how to get everybody improving whole systems. [p. 261]

Margaret Wheatley, of Brigham Young University, proposed in *Leadership and the New Science* (1992) the need to apply the new paradigms of chaos theory, quantum mechanics, and evolutionary biology to an understanding of organizations. Changing culture in corporations has become so popular that managers and executives are using such terms as "paradigm shift" in newspaper interviews, and President Clinton and Vice President Gore convene meetings of executives and labour leaders to discuss ways of reinventing government and developing new patterns of labour–management cooperation.

All of these strategies emphasize a sharing of experience among all of the participants. The experience comes first, and then participants are encouraged to describe how they understand that experience. Through such a method, members are enabled to create a culture of inquiry and action in which all may participate.

> Even when small fragments of culture are elevated to aware- ness, they are difficult to change, not only because they are so personally experienced but because people cannot act or inter- act at all in any meaningful way except through the medium of culture. [Hall, 1966, p. 188]

I believe that we have been gratifyingly successful in the effort to improve organizations. I question, however, whether we may rightly call what we do changing the culture. I suggest that there are three conditions that must be met in order to change a culture.

1. The change must be relatively enduring, resulting in a stable pattern of basic assumptions.
2. A culture requires a shared experience and pattern of percep- tion.
3. Since culture hides as much as it reveals, and since it hides the most important things, there must be a means to uncover un- conscious processes and make them available for thought.

Too often the culture change lasts only so long as the chief executive continues to support the changes. Wheatley (1992) has written:

> Why do so many organizations feel dead? Why do projects take so long, develop ever-greater complexity, and yet so often fail to achieve any truly significant results. ... Why does change itself, that event we're all supposed to be "managing", keep drowning us, relentlessly reducing any sense of mastery we might possess? And why have our expectations for success diminished to the point that often the best we hope for is

staying power and patience to endure the disruptive forces that appear unpredictably in the organizations where we work? [p. 1]

These new cultures, or "minicultures" as De Mare (De Mare, Piper, & Thompson, 1992) calls them, are too often fragile, as any one of us who has revisited a former client organization has seen. Even after a very successful consultation—which included staff development and management training, culminating in a search conference that I conducted in 1989, and which has led to a new employee-developed mission statement, facilities plans, programme plans, and a host of other excellent improvements—I recently heard employees of that organization say: "Things never change around here."

About a decade ago, some social scientists from America were invited to Yugoslavia to work with a number of communities to improve their industrial democracy. In particular, they led workshops that demonstrated how various ethnic and social groups could be melded together for greater understanding and productivity, and this appeared to be a model for progress. It has since become apparent that the splits in the former Yugoslavia are ancient and immutable, an intrinsic element of the cultures of the region.

A much more light-hearted illustration of this problem comes from a cartoon that a student gave me as I was teaching the virtues of Deming and TQM. In it, a chief executive was shown standing at a conference table with a group of his subordinates. The caption was: "I'm not satisfied with our progress in driving out fear, so if you don't drive out all the fear by next week you're all fired." It is an obvious case where the old paradigm takes over even from the conscious mind of the new.

The second condition is that the culture requires a shared experience and pattern of perception. Edward T. Hall, the anthropologist, wrote more than a generation ago that since culture moulds experience, members of different cultures do not even share the same experience of common events (Hall, 1966). Deborah Tannen, a linguist, has written in her popular book, *You Just Don't Understand* (1990), that "male–female conversation is cross cultural communication" (p. 42), suggesting that men and women are members of different cultures who do not share the same experience.

Richard J. Bates (1987) rejects the idea that there can be a unity of interests or culture in an organization. He claims that attempts to improve culture are ideological forms of control, which only serve the interests of elites against the interests of workers. Writing about state schools, he claims that those in affluent neighbourhoods have a market relationship with constituents, which enables students to develop the skills and knowledge needed in the prevailing culture. Schools in poorer areas are bureaucracies that mainly disrupt and disconfirm the basic experience of the students. While the children of the affluent are graded on a relative scale of success, the poorer ones are labelled as losers, save for a few talented individuals who are allowed to rise up. Bates is critical of cultural interventions because, he claims, they are strategies that favour the interests of the corporation and its leaders. These cultural elites may not be (indeed, probably are not) consciously imposing their will on the workers—it just happens.

The third condition was also identified by Hall (1966), who pointed out that culture hides as much as it reveals, and it hides the most important parts.

It is because the culture both creates our own ability to know and is outside of awareness that it has been found so difficult to change by conscious choice. Cosgrove (reported in Hart, 1991), in a study of leadership succession in schools, found that new and old principals and teachers could neither describe nor agree on the cultural values, norms, unspoken rules, assumptions, or beliefs in their workplace, and yet they claimed that others shared these with them.

Because the boundaries among various cultural systems are fluid, a change in one has the likelihood of unanticipated consequences in others. Even the most experienced leaders of nations are taken by surprise as a Berlin Wall goes down and Germany is reunited in a matter of weeks, or when the world's economy slips into a long recession that does not obey the old rules.

Another example of the unanticipated consequence arises out of the emphasis upon greater worker participation and fewer layers of bureaucracy. When coupled with the effects of a worldwide economic recession, the unanticipated consequence resulted in the possible extinction of middle management—the group, at least in the United States, that has experienced the downsizing of corporations most severely. Ironically, just as we have been emphasizing that greater worker loyalty can be gained through participation, the greater participation has led to a lowered need for loyal workers.

I suspect that we may have here instances of the so-called butterfly effect, in which minute differences in the input of a system rapidly escalate into enormous differences in output. This is a characteristic of systems that almost achieve a steady state but actually are aperiodic and therefore never quite repeat themselves (Gleick, 1987, p.22).

Another way in which the culture hides important elements arises out of the nature of groups. Part of the reason that there is chaos internal to the group as it seeks to adjust to the environment is because there is a corresponding chaos inherent in our experience of the external world. As the great 1993 Mississippi River flood demonstrated once more, the environment usually breaks whatever promises its subsystems thought had been made. The potential for both enormous power and apparent treachery of the environment thus elicits hatred and fear. Managing such unwanted feelings is one of the functions of culture. A primary means of managing them is to keep them hidden. Hirschhorn (1988) describes how some bank managers, in an attempt to create a non-bureaucratic culture, created a punishing and psychologically dangerous work climate to replace an anxiety-binding bureaucracy, by projecting the managers' anxiety onto the lowest-level workers. Projection is the way we hide from ourselves.

Much has been written about the organizational socialization of new workers and new leaders. A text that I use in classes in organizational behaviour (Hart, 1991) relates how socialization of new members is governed by a psychological contract already in existence. The whole effort of the study is to develop a way to make this contract conscious. Hart maintains that "organizations . . . protect against intrusion of new members, values, and beliefs by routinization and through formal and informal social mechanisms, one of which is socialization" (p. 469).

New members, new values, new beliefs, new cultural norms, coming as they do from the environment, elicit hatred and fear. A group's culture is won at great cost to its members. It has chosen a pattern of basic assumptions at a cost of confusion and suffering. It has had to develop rituals to bind up hurt feelings and tenuous relationships. It has created artifacts to symbolize other compromises. Eventually, it works out a structure of roles and dynamics to contain the chaos.

A group can respond in two ways to such an intrusion. On the one hand, it may treat an intruder with resentment borne out of a sense of, "if only you knew how much we have suffered". The group will then be tempted to inflict ritual suffering on the newcomer through initiation or hazing. "You must know what it has been like to suffer as we have suffered before you may properly be included as one of us." Another form may be to project into the newcomer, or the new idea, the unwanted feelings of hatred reserved for invaders [I am indebted to Yvonne Agazarian for the development of these ideas.]

To summarize, I believe that a true change of culture requires three conditions to be fulfilled: that the changes be enduring and not transitory; that they have a shared experience and pattern of perception; and that there be a means to tap into the hidden dimension of the culture.

I do not know what to say about the first condition—that of bringing about enduring change—except to suggest that we keep trying. I do believe that the change should, at a minimum, outlast the leader who introduces it. The second element—that of common experience and perception—is one that is being dealt with partially through worker participation and search conferences.

Weisbord's formula of "getting everybody to improve whole systems" does meet this condition. I suspect that it is the development of a common culture rather than the institution of democracy and power equalization that is the more important element in organizational improvement. Democracy and openness are important not just for themselves but because they make it possible for participants to work through their own imported assumptions to a new synthesis of shared assumptions.

I believe that social dreaming may help both here and in making the third, hidden dimension available. Dreams are the language of the purposely hidden. The challenge facing one who wishes to change an existing culture is how to reach the unconscious life of the organization. Because the cultures are embedded in one another, and because the elements not digested are projected into others, I wish to propose the hypothesis that the social dream can be a means to tap into the deeper levels where sharing can occur.

I have been greatly influenced by my own experiences as participant and staff member in the social dreaming programmes led by Lawrence, but how this might be applied has been in question. I do not suspect that executives or managers will be scheduling social dreaming matrices any time soon. Yet I have been attempting to discover how social dreaming might help our attempts to facilitate change in cultures, and to understand how it would do so.

The following is an attempt at understanding. I was asked to lead an adult forum class in my church, on the announced topic of "Social Dreams, Parables, and Faith". Participants were asked to come to the forum with their dreams and with a favourite parable of Jesus. While they were not schooled in group relations, this parish is located in an upper-middle-class neighbourhood, so participants were generally well educated and well adjusted, from the ranks of the professions and management. After a first meeting in which they tended to report recurring dreams (in my experience, this often occurs), we began to listen to dreams.

I had speculated that we might be able to treat parables as being similar to dreams. This was based partly on a technique used by the theologian Walter Wink (1973), in which parables are read as if they were dreams and students are encouraged to treat each element in the parable as though it were a part of oneself, much as in Gestalt therapy.

The first parable, presented as a favourite by a participant, was that of the sower and the seed (Mark 4:39):

> "A sower went out to sow, and it happened that as he sowed some fell along the footpath; and the birds came and ate it up. Some fell on rocky ground, where it had little soil, and it sprouted quickly because it had no depth of earth; but when the sun rose it was scorched, and as it had no root it withered away. Some fell among thistles; and the thistles grew up and choked the corn, and it produced no crop. And some of the seed fell into good soil, where it came up and grew, and produced a crop, and the yield was thirtyfold, sixtyfold, even a hundredfold."

It was difficult for the participants, solid Presbyterians, to imagine themselves as the sower, the seed, the rocky ground, the sun, the thistles, and so forth using the technique suggested by Wink. They believed that they already knew the meaning of this parable: the sower was Christ, the seed The Word, and it was for them to be good soil. As we struggled, it was suggested that perhaps it was Christ who was the sower, the seed, the rocky ground, the sun that withers. Then one member said: "Since we are dealing with social dreams, perhaps this was a social dream for the people of Israel. After all, they had been buffeted about like the seeds in the parable."

This insight has led me to re-examine what parables are and what function they serve. I propose to adopt an analysis based on the work of John Dominic Crossan, Professor of Religious Studies at DePaul University in Chicago, in a book entitled *The Dark Interval* (1988).

Crossan uses a structuralist analysis based on the idea that human beings are limited by language and therefore by story. While we may be able to transcend a particular story, we cannot get outside of story itself. It is interesting that while Crossan is a theologian writing in that context, there has been a parallel emphasis at recent meetings of the conferences of organizational behaviour scholars and teachers in the United States on the importance of telling the story to understand organizational dynamics.

The outer limits of story, according to Crossan, are myth and parable. At one limit is myth, which creates worlds. A parable, which stands at the opposite limit from myth, thwarts and undercuts the world presented by the myth and challenges the expectations of the hearer.

> Myth has a double function: the reconciliation of an individual contradiction and, more important, the creation of a belief in the permanent possibility of reconciliation. Parable also has a double function, which opposes that double function of myth. The surface function of parable is to create contradiction within a given situation of complacent security but, even more unnervingly, to challenge the fundamental principle of reconciliation by making us aware of the fact that we made up the reconciliation. [Crossan, 1988, p. 40]

If it is important to use dreams to work through issues in our individual lives, then it must also be important to use them to work through life in community. Dreams enable us to get at the hidden dimensions of experience, where culture has placed the most important things.

To create a culture requires the telling of a story which will function as a myth. The structure of the myth involves an opposition between two issues that cannot be mediated. The myth presents fictional characters, which can bring about a resolution or create a possibility. It also gives reassurance that the resolution will be eternal.

We can recall many examples of such a use of story to function as a founding myth for an organization. Colonel Sanders, like Robert Bruce, tried six or seven times before he succeeded in founding an empire, and in both cases the virtues of persistence became a part of the culture of the organization. Leaders of corporations appropriate the language of world-creating myth when they speak of the vision or the mission of the firm. They attempt to infuse this mission with emotion, they relate it to the historic mission pioneered by the founder, and they spend countless dollars and hours devising the right corporate symbol or logo. It is questionable whether a culture was actually created in these cases. The prevailing cultural environment was still at work. Important elements were still hidden from view.

The difficulty is that the dream is usually one that the leader seeks to impose upon the followers. The CEO has no way of knowing what others are dreaming, yet, as Beradt showed in *The Third Reich of Dreams* (1968), there have been many who have the same dreams with the same themes without knowing that they share these dreams.

I suspect that social dreams function not as myths, but as parables. This is more problematic, since parables express a critique of the world. However, to change an organization's culture involves the manager or consultant in such a critique.

As we have seen, the culture in place is a means of guarding the group against the intrusion of a new idea or person. A direct approach, even when done with great sensitivity, will arouse unconscious hatred, but these feelings, being most important, will be hidden from everyone.

Parable, as its name indicates, is indirect. In parable, the hearer expects one thing to be given, but what happens is the reverse of what the hearer expects. Parable subverts the world created by the myth (Crossan, 1988, p. 50). One result may be the possibility of a new myth and a changed culture, but the change will more likely be developmental than permanent.

Dreams often have this effect. In the Acts of the Apostles there is the account of a dream that St. Peter had while in a trance. He dreamed that *a great cloth descended from the sky filled with all manner of living creatures. He was commanded by a voice to kill and eat, but he demurred since he had never eaten any unclean or profane thing. The voice told him that he should not count unclean what God counts clean.* This led him to welcome the Roman, Cornelius, into the new faith. It was a parabolic dream that turned the movement from a small cult, which might have remained as an offshoot of Judaism, into Christianity.

While it was not without controversy, the fact of that dream and the associations made around it by the primitive Christians did provide the conditions necessary to deal with the two concerns voiced by Hall. The expectations of the hearers were subverted. They had to think differently about what they were doing. They all had a dream, which came out of the hidden region of the being.

Dream as parable appears to me to be consistent with the working hypothesis that Lawrence offers for social dreaming programmes (1991). This hypothesis asserts that we must get away from the political process of salvation to a politic of revelation. Most consultancy and action research has used the power of knowledge and expertise to "save" workers from their tribulations. Lawrence has proposed a politics of revelation in which people can interpret their own experience and "accept the surprise of their revelations". (This statement is taken from the brochure for the Third U.S. Program for Social Dreaming and Life in Organizations and Communities sponsored by the New York Centre of the A. K. Rice Institute.)

The good church members who already knew what the parable taught were examples of the politics of salvation. For them, the parable had been transformed into another form of story that Crossan calls an apologue, a teaching story, to be used for guidance. The parable is thus robbed of its power to surprise and transform.

Two other dreams, one from that church forum and another from the latest American programme of social dreaming, illustrate the parabolic nature of social dreams. The first was a dream reported by a woman who started the session by saying that while her favourite is the parable of the talents, the dream that she had did not involve the use of any of her own talents. In the dream, *she was asked by the father of a handicapped boy, whom she treats in her role as occupational therapist in a school for the handicapped, to help him by seeing that the boy gets to his classroom. His teacher is not there to take the boy directly. The boy is heavy, and she is not supposed to carry such a heavy weight for any period of time. The place is not the usual school, but a very confusing building with many corridors, and she has difficulty getting her bearings in unfamiliar places.* The association that we made is with the Presbyterian Church in the United States. It is undergoing great stress, with bitter controversies regarding the ordination of homosexuals, a precipitous decline in membership and revenues, and a loss of spiritual direction. Carrying the Son for the Father is too great a burden, we are in a maze, and there is no teacher (Bible, tradition, clergy appear to have lost their authority).

The second is a dream offered by a businessman at the social dreaming programme. He had expressed his concern about the situation of the United States, wondering whether we are responsible for being recipients of a mirage. The country is bankrupt yet it is financing a myth (the enormous military establishment), while others are competing with us as never before. Later, he reported a dream in which *he was driving his automobile around the back of a shopping centre. The buildings were placed so close to a hill that it had been cut away, so there was a high cliff of dirt there. He made three left turns until he was driving slowly along the front. A friend of his, who is very fat, weighing perhaps 400 pounds, stepped out of the grocery store with two large bags of groceries in his arms. The friend is always trying to lose weight. The businessman did not want to embarrass the fat man with the groceries, so he drove slowly by without looking at him. He noticed, however, as he passed by, that the fat man's face was ashen-gray and appeared to be a concrete mask. As he drove on, he looked in the rear-view mirror and saw the fat man wheel about and give the Nazi salute.* I view that as a parable of the American economy.

In this chapter, I have attempted to show that if we are to change the culture of organizations we must go more deeply into the shared experience of its members. Furthermore, it is necessary to create conditions by which individuals may share both the experience and the perception of events. This shared experience must be able to get at the hidden elements of the culture to make them available. I have hypothesized that the experience of social dreaming has the effect of assisting groups of individuals within organizations, departments, and public groups to experience new revelations of the hidden dimension.

CHAPTER NINE

Social dreaming as a tool of consultancy and action research

W. Gordon Lawrence

> We are such stuff as dreams are made on;
> and our little life is rounded with a sleep.
>
> *The Tempest*, Act IV, Sc. 1, 156–158

> I will get Peter Quince to
> write a ballad of this dream.
> It shall be call'd 'Bottom's
> Dream," because it hath no
> bottom.
>
> *A Midsummer Night's Dream*, Act IV, Sc. 1, 220–222

Action research, the unconscious, and dreaming

When I worked at the Tavistock Institute, there was no frame of reference with which to incorporate dreams into thinking about action research and consultancy. Nevertheless, there were experiences that caused me to start to think. In 1975, for instance, I was interviewing managers as part of an action research study of management development in companies in Britain. One manager volunteered that he had a repeated dream, which was that *he had to come to work each day through a graveyard, and no matter which route he took he always had to pass through a cemetery*. The associations we had in the interview were that his particular company was going to enter into a financial crisis that could be terminal. He felt depressed because most of his colleagues were denying this probability. It led me, subsequently, to think about the mortality of individual managers and the place of the idealization of careers in the lives of individuals. As important was the fantasy that the business enterprise was immortal, in that it would exist forever. This seemed to be a shared fantasy that role-holders projected into the business "in the mind", irrespective of the current trading and commercial realities. Whatever uncertainties they had of the future were projected into the business, which acted as a "container", and they could introject, in turn, certainty.

The other example comes from about 1980, when I had an interview with a civil servant in the then Department of Employment. At one point he seemed to slip into a reverie and said that he had a repeated dream that *England in the future would become a nation of city-states as in Mediaeval Italy*. He himself was of Italian descent, so that might have explained his metaphor. What he said as he developed the idea of communities being in some kind of tension and self-protective posture, if not in actual conflict, echoed with experiences of living in Britain at the time. We had begun to experience yet another recession, and already people were beginning to be unemployed. The difference from the past was that it was the members of the traditionally safe managerial occupations who were now vulnerable. There was a sense of social classes defining themselves more sharply and of different racial groups self-consciously emerging in England with each of them having the characteristics of a beleaguered minority. Their anxiety for the future fuelled a growing sense that people had to be more and more narcissistically preoccupied with their concerns for survival (Lawrence, Bain, & Gould, 1996). It was with these and similar experiences, coupled with what I had learned in my own psychoanalysis, that I realized that dreaming could be an area for exploration in the context of action research and consultancy projects.

The backgound to social dreaming

The history of how social dreaming emerged has been described elsewhere (see chapter one; see also Lawrence, 1991). To date, the work has been done in the context of social dreaming programmes convened for that purpose, and these programmes have allowed my consultant colleagues and myself to understand further the processes involved in social dreaming in the context of a matrix.

One programme has been pivotal in helping to shape social dreaming as a tool of action research and consultancy. This programme, entitled "Social Dreaming as Memoirs of the Future: An Action Research Project", has been held for three years at the William Alanson White Institute in New York. There the members of the organizational development course are students in an institution that has a continuous life, so there is a sense of a community of shared interest which lasts for a number of years. It has been clear from these particular programmes that social dreaming can be used to enable participants to clarify the nature of the work relations amongst them and the transference and countertransference issues that inevitably occur between the faculty and the students. By exploring the content of members' dreams, conflicts, which sometimes have been too painful to surface in everyday discourse, have come to be understood and resolved through the process of amplification. So social dreaming started to have an action research dimension because it was seen that the dreams could be used to illumine the communal life of the students and the faculty, at the very least.

Social dreaming does not question the use and value of dreams in the classic, psychoanalytic tradition but, like Bion's work on groups, affirms that dreams have also a social dimension, though there needs to be a dreamer to give expression to them. The primary task of a social dreaming matrix is usually: "To associate to one's own and others' dreams as made available to the matrix so as to make links and find connections."

Excerpts from a social dreaming matrix

For the past four years, I have organized a seminar for the president and managing directors of a group of companies. In 1994 I introduced a social dreaming matrix to the seminar. The companies are all involved in trade by mail order, and each has a substantial turnover running into millions of pounds. All the companies are experiencing some difficulties because of their respective national economies, increased competition, and a general downturn in consumer spending. The phrase that emerged during the seminar to capture their current situation was that they conduct business in a *"Casino des incertitudes"*.

I introduced social dreaming because I felt that awakening and speaking with their unconscious through dreams might help them to think how they could engage with business uncertainty in a more confident way. I was trying also to find ways into revealing what "unthought known(s)" (Bollas, 1987) might be present in the group of companies. Consultants or action researchers work in institutions where the role-holders face both the private troubles and public issues, to borrow C. Wright Mills's phrase, engendered by living and managing in contemporary, unpredictable environments. The role-holders are living in what they experience and understand to be a real world full of real problems. They relate to these with a nagging fear that a wrong decision will bring catastrophic consequences—an institutional world of chaos. Consequently, they think and act very often from a psychic position of defending themselves from the psychotic anxiety that would be engendered by chaos. This results in the political fabrication of organizational systems to hold this anxiety at bay. At the same time, role-holders know that they are participating in what I call a "rational madness"—that is, that the structure and form of the organization when examined does not make sense, particularly in circumstances where events and happenings in the external environment are lurching from one discontinuity to another. Often, however, this cannot be thought of and articulated, because of the fear that there will be chaos if the form of the organization is deconstructed.

Since Christopher Bollas's formulation of the "unthought known", action researchers and consultants, led by David

Armstrong, have come to see that an investigatory aspect of their work is the

> ... bringing into view at an organizational level of something known in the organization, known in the emotional and physical and perhaps imaginal life of the organization which has resisted formulation: something primary and ordinary, that is lived, but only as a shadow. And once formulated, once brought towards thought paradoxically creates a difference which makes a difference to how every decision, policy, action is understood. It does not make things easier; it does not show a client what to do. But it discloses meaning: introduces the client, as it were, to the organization-in-himself and himself-in-the organization. And this disclosure sets a new agenda. [Armstrong, 1994b, p. 5]

This commitment to revealing the "unthought known" is consistent with the view that action research and consultancy in the original Tavistock tradition is grounded in the "politics of revelation" rather than those of "salvation" (Lawrence, 1994). Revelation of the unconscious functioning of groups, institutional life, and life as it is lived in societies that exist in the context of an eco-systemic environment has emerged over the years as the agenda of action research. This has to be contrasted with consultancy as "salvation"—that is, as a social variant of the "rescue phantasy" that can operate in the therapeutic situation when the practitioner is caught up in trying to offer salvation to the client. The "politics of salvation" are geared to saving the "client" organization from its problems or, for instance, to expertly introducing the latest technology, such as a new IT system; the politics of revelation, on the other hand, are centred on the idea that the clients themselves can take responsibility and assert authority to disentangle the nature of realities in order to manage themselves in their roles within their particular systems. The consultant working in such a revelatory mode has a preoccupation with the infinite, the unconscious, with socially induced psychosis, with the unthought known, with the social phenomena that rational madness brings forth.

The dream is the classic link between the finite and the infinite, the conscious and the unconscious. "A night dream is a spontaneous symbolic experience lived out in the inner world during sleep. Such dreams are composed of a series of images, actions, thoughts, words, and feelings over which we seem to have little or no conscious control" (Savary, 1984). Dreaming makes the dreamer aware that what is taken for granted in waking life can be made non-sense of during sleep when rationality is suspended. Action research, which is postulated on the revelation of the unconscious mind, would be expected to have made use of dreams and dreaming. Even though the methodology is based on psychoanalytic thinking, access to the role-holders' dreams has never been part of the discourse of action research. This, probably, is because in the popular Western imagination dreams have come to be understood to be a personal, private experience rarely to be shared except with a therapist who would have the skill to "interpret" them.

Returning to the seminar: each day, mostly in the mornings, we had a social dreaming matrix that lasted for an hour. Social dreaming was introduced with some trepidation, for I was unsure what would be realized and how it would evolve. I always have an anxiety before a matrix opens that no dreams will be made available, but on this occasion I had the added anxiety that dreaming would be rejected as being not relevant to the participants' work. The title of the seminar was "Memoirs of the Future". It was conducted in French. Working with me was a young French manager, Dominique Guisiano, marketing director of a chain of retail clothing shops, who had been a participant at a previous week-long programme of social dreaming in England.

I have made a selection of the dreams with his help to try to illustrate the potential of social dreaming by showing that people with pressing business problems can benefit from the experience. The selection is as representative of the whole experience of the matrix as we can make it. In this account, I wish to preserve confidentiality, so contributions are anonymous.

The first matrix opened with one participant saying that he felt angry at being present in a seminar on a Sunday evening. (The seminar began on a Sunday and ended on the following Wednesday after the final social dreaming matrix from 9 to 10 a.m.) There were some observations made on the nature of dreaming, and some participants wondered whether in fact they did dream. They concluded that they dreamed more when they were on holiday, and particularly when staying at high altitudes, than when they were at work. One manager, who had a dream of being on an escalator, expressed the doubt about the value and possible risks of dreaming. He had the feeling of being off-balance and that he was always trying to keep in balance. It was not an unpleasant feeling, but, at the same time, it was not a pleasure. I took it that the escalator symbolized links between waking and dreaming, reality and dream, between the conscious and the unconscious, which is always putting one off-balance but, ideally, could be in a symbiont relationship.

Another manager followed by saying that normally he did not remember his dreams, but he had had one the night before, and when he awoke he was able after some effort to recall some elements. His dream, he said, was in relation to the catalogue of his company. (The catalogue for a mail order company is the key selling tool, and thus its quality is critical.) *There was a fashion presentation that was taking place on the gangway and the ladder of a boat. The presentation was being photographed. The feeling of the place was of elegance, with a lot of people present. It was, however, cold. The people present were fashion designers, and the atmosphere was a little mad, even bizarre. There was a lot of light from the sun and much movement among the people present.* The dreamer ended his description by saying that they were not dealing with issues of fashion in his company.

I was intrigued that one of the first dreams should be about work, and I assumed that the gangway [*passerolle*] symbolized the catalogue issued by the company, with its marketing strategies to sell its goods to potential customers either on the "boat" or the "quay". In actuality, the company has an attractive catalogue and even has what are called "best sellers", but the amount of turnover needed is not yet present, so it is therefore very worrying for all the people in the company. There is stress in the company, and a sense of persecution has grown because of their comparative lack of success. The market is a cold place in reality. (The theme of water was to reappear in subsequent dreams of the matrix and can be assumed to be a reference to the unconscious.)

The fact that the act of dreaming was engaging participants and causing them to reflect on its nature was made clear by one participant who described that he had two kinds of dreams: first, a *rêve lancinant*; second, a *rêve d'envol*. The first kind of dream, he said, was like listening to music which goes on for a long time, and it occurs when he has difficulties. The second kind of dream happens during periods of social excitement or when he is experiencing good, affective relationships. This kind of dream he likened to a bird flying from island to island. He added that he had not had the second kind of dream when he was appointed a managing director. Someone, at this point, observed that we create a story with our dreams, perhaps to restore ourselves.

A dream was given about a group consisting of members of the seminar.

All were visiting the Souk in Marrakech. It was full of colour and smells. The dreamer said that it was a very rich and vivid dream for him. At the edge of the Souk there were wooden barriers. Alongside one of these barriers was a collection of furniture made from olive trees. The wood was rich, heavy, and colourful. The barriers halted the group. They wanted to go out by the left because they wished to go and visit another place or do something else; from the left, children appeared, and the air was filled with an extraordinary smell. A small open-top car appeared. [Later we established that it was an "Alpine", made by Renault a few years ago.] The car had bumpers, but they were dented on the left-hand rear side. [The significance of references to "left" (gauche) in this and subsequent dreams was not clear, except in the sense of either "awkward" or "sinister".] By the car was a salesman who had blond hair. The dreamer kept wondering if he was honest but he had the look of a Norseman so he felt that he must be trustworthy. By the side of the dreamer was Nicholas, his son.

The car transforms into the back wheel and the rear of a motorcycle. In front is the head of a dog, called a chien des avalanches [St. Bernard]. The dog is licking Nicholas, who reciprocates by licking the dog. The dreamer does not like this, because the dog may not be clean. He says so to Nicholas, who replies, "I have the money and I need two places."

The dream was followed by what the participants called a "flash" (this was their word). This dreamer had two. The first one was *Ta foi t'a sauve*—"Faith saves one"—and the theme of faith had been running through the seminar in other events. His second was that he was wondering where Lawrence was to put any new books into his library. We were sitting in a large room in which there were a few thousand books around the walls.

This dream had considerable importance, but the full meaning is not yet clear. As the associations were being offered it was established that the barriers were formed from cross beams shaped like a cross of St. Andrew. The top executive of the group, who was not present, is called Andrew, and the role of the dreamer is to work closely with him, arranging, for example, the acquisition of new companies (attractive olive-wood furniture?) and selling those that are no longer viable. The theme of "alpine" occurs twice. There is the motor-car and the dog. The company has strong associations with Switzerland. The motor-car transforms into something else. Is this one of the problems of mail order, that the old methods are no longer working with the same efficacy? The dog is a benign and helpful one. Does this represent how companies should treat their customers? What is the relation of the dreamer to his work in the companies in the group, as indicated by his son who has the money. Where are the two places? Is the relationship purely a calculative, instrumental one, and what is the place of faith in business? The Souk, fairly obviously, could symbolize the market environment, but it was pointed out to me that Souk is also a *bordel*. Since this word is often used to describe a total mess or shambles, it might mean something about the state of the market.

I jump to a later dream in the sequence. *The dreamer is walking on the left side of a road. Coming towards him is his company president, who is also on the left of the road. The right-hand side of the road is piled high with stones. The dreamer is not sure if these stones are the result of a rockfall, or if they are waiting to be used in the rebuilding of the road. He says that he is not sure if they are there as a result of destruction or if they are waiting for use in construction. The road itself is well marked, but is the line marking the centre of the road or marking the edge of it?*

The dreamer gives his second dream, which is erotic. *Along with another fellow, he meets two gorgeous women. There is a little house that is a sauna.* He says he cannot give the end of the dream— whether because he forgot it or out of delicacy, I am not sure. He remarks that in the hotel he is sleeping in an old-fashioned iron bed that has brass balls on the bed ends. All night as he moves in bed they go "kling-kling".

This dream echoes the actual political situation of the dreamer as a new managing director working with the president, who, up to now, has also held the role of managing director. We thought that the stones on the right—one of the president's names is Pierre (*pierre* = stone)—represented the company, which has experienced a downturn in trading. Could the company be turned around— that is, is reconstruction possible, or is it in a disastrous, ruinous state? Where are the limits to any future growth of the company? The unasked questions around for all the members of the seminar were, can the new managing director work with the president? Will they have a confrontational, conflictual relationship or work in harmony? Who is the other fellow in the erotic dream—the president?

Another dreamer is on the gangway of a boat. *He cannot see anything because there is fog, but everyone assures him that when the weather is good it is a very nice view.* Our association was to the present state of the companies, seeing the gangway, again, as the commercial link between the companies and their customers. While matters now may be bad, perhaps better trading conditions will come when the fog lifts.

Again, I jump in the sequence. The other consultant says he has had a dream in which *everyone is at a big table with large quantities of food. There are a lot of people around it. He feels joyful but worried because nobody is available for serving the food.* Later, he and I talked, and we thought that the dream was a reflection of his anxiety of how I managed the seminar. My aim was to create conditions for thinking and thoughts to be available, and so I rarely intervened in events except to press this aim forward. By the dream bringing the anxiety forward, we were able to talk about our work relationship and the place of reflective "containment" in an educational setting.

Another dreamer said that he dreamt of *working with a woman director.*

> There are about fifteen people around a big table, which he thought was located in the building of the company in Paris where he had worked before. The purpose of the meeting is the presentation of a collection of clothes. A woman who is either a director or the owner's wife is managing this. In the dream, she is aged about 40 and he is 30.
> She says: "I found these tiles [carreaux de sol] in the selection room." Another women replies, "They would be perfect for me."
> "May I add them to your purchases?", asks the vendeuse.

The dreamer was very angry because these tiles belonged to the fabric of the building and were not part of the collection for sale, and he said that while he was employed in the company nothing would be taken from the enterprise. He realized that he was the guardian of l'ethique, and that he saw this woman as an enemy because she was always saying the contrary to him.

In many ways, this dream expressed the dreamer's dilemmas in the group of companies, in which he often feels in disagreement about the long-term policies of the selling and the acquisition of companies. He is very concerned that the French group is partly owned by a German shareholder, and he has anxieties that ultimately the French group will become, in effect, a German commercial colony and then no one will know what is the real identity of the French group.

A subsequent dreamer recounts his dream. *He is sailing down a river in a boat. The torrent is very powerful and there are rocks. While he is travelling in the boat he is working on the translation and explanation of a fable by Goethe. When his work is completed another manager, who is also in the dream matrix, reads his text to an audience.* [To add a note, the reader is the most recent appointee to the managing director role.] *He is not present in the boat going down the river.* In reality, the dreamer is the most senior director of human resources for the group of companies.

For French people, it would be La Fontaine who is the obvious author of fables, but we assumed that Goethe represented the other substantial shareholder in the group of companies. Perhaps the dreamer's role in the future would be to give explanations of German policy to French managers who would give voice to it and act on it?

In the last session of the social dreaming matrix, the other consultant said that he had had a dream in which *he found himself to be the only spectator and was not eating with the others.* He said that this might reflect perceptions of his role in the seminar.

Another dreamer said that he had a dream but in the dream *he experienced himself as conscious and awake. He is speaking to another managing director about a new marketing manager, who is being transferred from one company in the group to another.* [This was true.] *The dreamer finds himself saying that this marketing manager speaks English very well—indeed would have an A grade. The president reacts to this by saying: "You see, you don't have enough confidence in people. Leave me, I am going to read the Bible." He does so, and in the dream he is facing Lawrence, who is reading the Bible but in English.*

In the dream the president was reading the book of Baruch, which is not in the King James Version but does appear in the Apocrypha, having been excluded from the Protestant canon at the time of the Reformation. Baruch appears in French Bibles. As far as I have been able to check, Baruch was important for giving a message to the conquered people who were under Babylonian rule. He also saved the religious furnishings of the temple after a holocaust. The president is Catholic, and it is well-enough known that I am not. So I took it that the dream expressed something of the difficulty that the dreamer has in understanding why a French company president should have an English-speaking consultant. And what is the nature of the transference between them? Who has access to what kind of knowledge? The possible reason for the selection of Baruch was that it might express something of the "phenomenal" role of the president in the group—that is, trying to celebrate and maintain its French identity in an international context.

The next dream, which I will make the last in this account, was a fable of the "Fat Duke and the Little Vassal".

There is a town in which lives a Little Vassal. The Fat Duke comes to visit, and the Little Vassal welcomes him to the town. There is in the place a big armchair that could also be a throne, and it is used for that purpose on occasion. When the Little Vassal sits in the armchair the whole town is illuminated, and the longer he sits in the chair the more intense is the light. In order to have the very best light possible, it is suggested that the Fat Duke also should sit in the armchair with the Little Vassal.

While the two are sitting in the chair, the son of the Little Vassal, who is an architect, is installing a spiral, which is in the form of a mobile, to the ceiling of the room in which the Fat Duke and the Little Vassal are seated. It is a very innovative and attractive spiral. The Little Vassal finds that there are two ways to sit in the chair with the

Fat Duke. If the Little Vassal is on his own, he can make his body flat shaped—like a slice of bacon—and so spread himself over the greatest area of the chair to provide his fellow townspeople with even more light. When the Fat Duke is present, however, he finds that if he is not quick enough the Fat Duke sits on top of him and squashes him. When the Fat Duke is in the chair with him, he still has to shape himself like a slice of bacon but sitting upright like a piece of toast in a rack.

There is a terrible scream from outside with someone shouting, "Douleur, frustration, cholere!" [pain, frustration, anger]. *The dreamer says that the Little Vassal is very "sympa"* [empathic] *but the Fat Duke is "antipathetique"* [not very empathic]. *What the Little Vassal felt was great frustration and the experience of being made ashamed in front of his son, the architect, in the presence of the Fat Duke.*

This dream summarizes much of the frustrations and feelings of being in this group of companies—pain, frustration, and anger. I suspect that the Little Vassal and the Fat Duke represent the shareholders. All of this cannot be spoken about publicly, so it comes forward in the dreams and so falls into the domain of the "unthought known". The French–German axis tends to be construed in contemporary European terms that are fashionable. Furthermore, the differences between a French mode of managing and a German one are easily denied, because all the companies have the same work, structures, and methods, which are the universal ones of mail order. My speculation was that the mobile spiral might symbolize the DNA of the group, when DNA is represented as a double helix, and that the future, company successors (son as architect) might have to give the group a new identity, which, at present, could only hang suspended in space and time. The Fat Duke and the Little Vassal sitting on the throne symbolized the hidden struggle between the German and the French to control the companies in the future. This may well be shaming for older French managers in front of their younger compatriots. The Little Vassal could give light—leadership and employment—but it was assumed that the Fat Duke could give more if he added his bulk to the throne. The result, however, would be that the Little

French Vassal would have to be squashed or squeezed out. All this, as I have indicated, is known at some level in the organization, but it is never articulated through thought because it would result in role-holders having to think through the political version of the organization which they carry "in the mind" and their own psychic perception of themselves in that organization. Through the dreams, however, these issues have now been revealed.

I have given this lengthy, but nevertheless considerably shortened, extract from a sequence of dreams and associations in a matrix in order to give the feeling of what can happen when people with a shared work interest come together to dream socially. Essentially, I am trying to show that social dreaming can be used as one tool of action research, though always in conjunction with the other methods that have traditionally been used. In this way, the repertoire is extended.

Working hypotheses on social dreaming

As more and more colleagues have joined me in the activity of social dreaming since 1982, we have come to learn increasingly. The most important of these insights I present here in the form of working hypotheses.

1. The first hypothesis—that it is possible to have dreams that have a social content and significance—was substantiated through the experiences of the first social dreaming matrix in 1982. From the extract in the previous section, it can be seen that people in roles in companies do dream about themselves in role and in the context of their business, and they dream of issues and conflicts that often cannot be voiced and debated publicly.

2. The second hypothesis is that if the dreams were received in a group rather than a matrix there would be different social processes present. The mental space of a matrix is different from a group—not better or worse, but different. In a matrix, the dreams of the participants are the "currency". In a group it would be the nature of the relationships between the members.

In particular, transference and countertransference issues would be expected to be dealt with in the "here-and-now" of the group. By having a matrix, such issues come to be dealt with through the dreams—for example, the president and myself reading different Bibles, to cite from the sequence above. Indeed, colleagues' experience is that if such issues are discussed in the matrix, they are talked away and so rob the dreams of the residues on which to work.

There is, I shall take the opportunity to add here, what could be called a "meta" transference issue. One dreamer in an American matrix dreamt that *she had to swim between two islands. One was marked "Tavistock Group Relations" and the other "Social Dreaming". The writer was encouraging her to swim from the former to the latter.* This, in actuality, does not represent my position, because I see social dreaming as being—just as a previous innovation in group work, the Praxis Event (Lawrence, 1985), has been—a development of the Tavistock tradition of understanding unconscious social processes, suffused as they are with psychosis.

3. The third hypothesis is that the existence of a matrix to receive the dreams alters the nature of the dreams compared with a classic psychoanalytic situation. In short, a change in container alters the nature of what is contained, and so the content of social dreaming is different. The dreams recounted in this chapter probably would have been different had the participants been taking part as individuals in an analytic session.

4. The fourth hypothesis is that the idea of a matrix alters the nature of the thinking processes and of how meanings are arrived at by the participants. Whereas in a group the concern is to create a universe of meaning, since otherwise mutual understanding would be felt to be impossible, in a matrix a plethora of meanings can coexist for a particular dream. If one thinks about it, there are as many associations to a dream as there are participants in a matrix. In a matrix, it is possible to live with a multi-verse of meaning. It can be argued that such an experience is psychotic-like, but it may be that the desire to have one interpretation for an event or dream is also a manifes-

tation of psychosis. There can be a tyranny in pre-emptive interpretation. It is the act of mental association that is the creative element in social dreaming.

5. The fifth hypothesis is that social dreaming questions the notion that dreams are personal possessions. This is true in the psychoanalytic situation, to be sure, because of the nature of the dyadic relationship. In a matrix, people dream of the matrix and anticipate their experiences of it ("Will it be an unbalancing ride on an escalator?"). The idea of the "social" dream has led my colleagues and me to think that, just as Bion postulated that there are thoughts in search of a thinker, so there may be dreams in search of a dreamer.

6. The sixth hypothesis is that the dreams in a social dreaming matrix alert participants to the tragic aspects of life and intimate the horrendous that is to come. Often, such issues cannot be spoken of directly because they are so frightening. Examples come from American programmes, where a good deal has been surfaced through dreams as to what may happen to the country in the future. In the sequence I have offered in this chapter, the dream of the Little Vassal and the Fat Duke has tragic tones, and it may be that in the future of this particular group of companies the Little Vassal will be squashed flat like a slice of bacon.

7. The seventh hypothesis is that dreams experienced in a social dreaming matrix are a threat to ordinary awareness. The dream has its own logic, embedded in its manifest and latent content, which questions the rationality experienced in waking life. The logic of a dream, if accepted and followed, may question the illogicality of existing in contemporary civilizations and their institutions. As I have observed for years, often our organizations are an expression of "rational madness" as their role-holders strive to avoid the anxiety of psychosis. There is evidence since the very first matrix that what is unconsciously known about the institutions of the dreamers and the societies in which they live out their lives comes to be present in their dreams. While they may consciously make their knowledge absent in their waking lives, their experiences come to be present in their dreams. The dream gives the lie to ordinary awareness.

8. The eighth hypothesis is that social dreaming is a tool of action research that is in the making. I suspect that this process of becoming will be arrested by moves to convert social dreaming into an activity taking place in groups, because social dreaming in a matrix is very open-ended and difficult to tolerate (cf. Baird, 1994). To be a consultant to a matrix is to be never certain, always speculative. This is unlike being in a group, where, with what has become distortions of the Tavistock "technology", there is always the fantasy that one is right, at least some of the time. The dream, however, can be understood to be the almost undisturbed activity of the unconscious, and, as Freud pointed out, censorship—which is the activity of the conscious mind— can be used to forget dreams and so negate the insight of the unconscious. The method used to work with dreams in a social dreaming matrix needs to be congruent with a respect for the unconscious and alive to the possibility of censorship. At present, I think that there should be only sparse intervention by the consultant, and then only to lead into association so as to further the discovery of the meanings of dreams by participants. I try to have faith in the dream and faith that the dream carries its own meaning and interpretation enshrined in it.

9. The ninth hypothesis is that, provided we can remember our dreams, we can have confidence that we are in touch with our unconscious, and, if we can associate to them mentally, and use amplification, to find out their meanings, we are on speaking terms with our unconscious. If that is made possible, we can minimize the possibility of being caught up in psychotic-like social processes because we can speak with our own psychosis. The dream itself, it can be postulated, is a natural, primordial form of action research by the psyche, on the psyche, for the psyche to unravel its relations with the external world of other people and natural phenomena.

10. The tenth hypothesis is the most disturbing. Unamuno says that we ourselves are "a dream, a dream that dreams". There is sufficient evidence in the literature to show that inventors and discoverers dream what they are puzzling out. What we do in our daily lives may well be rehearsed during the time of dreaming. The Australian Aborigines refer to the "Dreamtime", a time

when the land and its features and its peoples and gods were dreamt into existence. If, however, we do not listen to our dreams and rely totally on our consciousness, we may be cutting ourselves off from the roots of our unconscious, both good and bad.

The social dreaming matrix that I have sketched in this chapter had an unexpected denouement. The managing directors left the seminar in France feeling that it had been a liberating experience in terms of thinking. All of them, I repeat, were facing exacting commercial challenges. All were competent and knew their *métier* intimately. Each had been able to give the others confidence that they had to be continually reinventing the business of mail order if their companies were to survive and prosper in the future. They had recognized that social dreaming would never give them a direct answer to the issues that they were facing, but that the experience of searching for meanings would have direct consequences on the way that they thought about problems.

One of them had mentioned during the seminar that he had lost a notebook that he had been keeping while he was waiting to take over his new role as managing director. He had been recording in the notebook his observations of the company, disentangling issues that he had to address and reasoning out decisions he had to make. He had lost the notebook before the seminar and could not find it anywhere. The others had commiserated with him on his loss. The night after the seminar he had a dream in which *he placed the notebook in the drawer of a black desk*. On awakening, he thought of black desks. He had one neither in his office nor his home. The only one he knew was that of the President, but it would have been unrealistic to place it there. As he thought about it, he remembered that the desk had been an antique one with a not entirely smooth surface to its top. He thought more and remembered that he had been in a hotel with such a desk. He telephoned the hotel, and the manager said, "Yes, we have your notebook, but we did not know to whom to mail it. We will send it to you!" And so the managing director was restored to his lost transitional object. Social dreaming may be useful, at least, for finding our "lost properties" that are contained in our dreams, even though—like Peter Quince—we may not always get to the bottom of them.

CHAPTER TEN

Simultaneity and parallel process: an on-line applied social dreaming matrix

Marc Maltz and E. Martin Walker

The unforeseeable outcomes of applying social dreaming to organizational systems are one characteristic of this open-ended process that stirs passions both for and against. This chapter invites associations and discussion from readers by describing a consultation (reorganization and downsizing) to a major manufacturer of entertainment media—once a family business and now a subsidiary of a large U.S.-based entertainment conglomerate—through the social dreaming matrix that accompanied it.

The chapter introduces a series of births or timelines from which the parallel work of a social dreaming matrix and an organizational consultation evolved. It is a guide to the events that became this work and a way of presenting data to the reader so that she or he may join the writers in the process of learning about the application of social dreaming to organizational processes. This data is offered here for discussion and learning in order that the reader can participate in what the writers believe is an open-ended process in which the meaning of this body of work will evolve.

The evolutions presented here are:

• The birth of a matrix
• The history of the consultation
• Significant events of this applied social dreaming matrix
• Learning, conclusions, and hypotheses

The birth of a matrix

Lawrence noted that "social dreaming has a long past but a short history" (1996b, p. 199). This history dates from the first matrix carried out at the Tavistock Centre (Lawrence & Daniel, 1982) and the subsequent theoretical shift in which social dreaming differentiated itself from existing psychoanalytic and socio-technical methods. This shift was to reject the need—in order to make sense of what was to occur in a group experience—for an analyst, consultant, or group "taker" in an interpretive role or an *a priori* theoretical framework. From the writers' point of view, this recapitulates the spirit of Wilfred Bion's *Experiences in Groups* (1961) from which are drawn so many insights into group and organizational dynamics. Although social dreaming has roots in Freudian, Kleinian, and Jungian psychoanalysis, much of Lawrence's inspiration came from the phenomena in Tavistock group relations conferences in which dreams often informed a group as to what was happening on an unconscious level, in a manner consistent with similar phenomena described at length by Jaques, Menzies, and many others (Lawrence, 1996).

Following the 1982 matrix, Lawrence further refined social dreaming technology and saw to the development of matrices all over the world (see chapter one). Tom Michael (1995) discussed how "the politics of revelation" (Lawrence, 1994) can interact with the formation of organization cultures in institutions, and he suggested that dreams act as parables that challenge existing organizational cultures by creating the possibility of a totally new one.

Lawrence convened the first social dreaming matrix in New York in 1993, the same year that Walker chartered an organization at New York University called "Inner Media", whose mission statement declared that individuals could use a combination of group (Cohn, 1969) and meditative methodologies to develop their own unique ways of "seeing things as they actually are in the here and now". The choice of the word media was derived from its tripartite definition as "the middle", "a nurturing field of organismic development", or "that through which information is carried to our senses".

The social dreaming project presented in this chapter was born from work at the William Alanson White Institute's (WAWI) Programme for Organizational Development and Consultation between 1993 and 1995. In March 1993. The WAWI hired and worked with Lawrence to apply his social dreaming method (Lawrence, 1991, 1996) to the programme itself. This was to be the first of three matrices that Lawrence was contracted for, the others being in February 1994 and February 1995. The event in March 1993 was Maltz's first experience of a social dreaming matrix; Walker joined this experience the following year.

The writers found the learning derived from social dreaming to be immediately useful in their independent work of finding and tapping the unconscious of groups. They were also struck by the manner in which dreams yield learning about the organization which enables certain data contained in an individual's conscious and/or unconscious to be spoken and worked with in the organization without the powerful and often negative effects (projective identification, transference and countertransference) experienced in both their group-relations and workplace experiences. A significant event proved to be the inclusion of social dreaming in the "Exploring Global Social Dynamics" conference in Lorne, Australia, in 1993. The preparation for the conference and for the WAWI programme's participation in it contributed to the thinking of the writers about ways in which this technique could be used in the workplace.

In September 1994, the writers began a conversation about dynamic consultation and social dreaming in an e-mail exchange. During this series, Walker offered a dream to which Maltz associated. Then, in October 1994, a study group was formed by the WAWI programme, in which students, alumni, and faculty entered into a dialogue about what was learned from the matrices, as a continuing action research project. At Maltz's suggestion, the study group entered into a social dreaming matrix, in which dreams were shared and associated to in the task of discussion and learning.

A subgroup of this study group (the writers and three women) began sharing dreams on-line on the Internet (via e-mail) in November 1994. During this time, discussions were held between the writers on the challenges inherent in forming social dreaming matrices on-line. This led to the observation that dreams and associations are both simultaneous (in their discovery by the individuals in the matrix) and sequential (in the order by which they are made available). These issues are discussed further later in the chapter. The subgroup was formed with the bounded task of discovering what could be learned about on-line matrices with a defined membership.

The writers' participation in the third matrix in Lawrence's contract with the programme, in February 1995, added to their experience of taking social dreaming to the workplace as a tool for organizational (dynamic) consultation. The WAWI study group continued their work in person and on-line until May 1995, at which point the group arranged to continue to meet on-line. In May, the group recorded a two-session dialogue centred on Lawrence's note to the programme following the February 1994 matrix, entitled "Social Dreaming as Memoirs of the Future—February, 1994".

During the summer months, dreams were offered and associated to by the subgroup mentioned above in an on-going e-mail matrix. At this time, Maltz was in the second year of a consultation to an organizational system (the entertainment media manufacturer, based in northeast Pennsylvania), in which action research and the dynamic understanding of organizational processes were aggressively pursued. A particular member of this organization, a protegé of Maltz's, showed increasing interest in dreaming and associating to dreams. In June, she and Maltz informally began sharing dreams and associations to inform their specific work experiences within her system. (Her organizational role, at this time, was an internal continuous improvement consultant.) Increasingly, dreams shared in the study group matrix by Maltz were "cc:'d" (i.e. simultaneously distributed electronically by e-mail) to this individual. Members of the study group had difficulty with this "inclusion", and a discussion ensued as to where the boundary of an on-line matrix begins and ends. The specific question raised (which remains) is: does an on-line matrix get formed by those the dream is initially addressed "to" (as in the "to" of an e-mail) and the subsequent associations and dreams that follow as posted, or is it formed by whoever receives the dream?

In September 1995 (after the WAWI programme discontinued the social dreaming study group due to lack of funds), Walker shared a dream on e-mail which Maltz experienced as, among other things, a dream about the consultation that he was involved with in Pennsylvania and as a consultation to it. Maltz asked Walker's permission to share the dream with his client. In November 1995, Maltz's client responded with a powerful association to the dream concerning events transpiring in the consultation. Walker's dream became a bridge from the earlier matrices formed in and at the WAWI programme to the matrix that is the focus of this chapter. The matrix was thus borne on-line by the two writers and the client member (CM).

A boundary and role negotiation ensued in which the differentiation of role and task were as follows: the client assumed the role of member of the matrix and was to share (i.e. post) dreams and associations from herself and others in the organization, identifying the source. (During the life of the matrix, five additional members—four female and one male—participated and shared dreams through CM.) Maltz took up the role of member of the matrix and concentrated on linking the dreams and associations (including his own) to the consultation; Walker managed the boundaries of the matrix, consulted to it, and shared his dreams and associations. The task of the on-line matrix was to learn about this particular system from dreaming and associating to the dreams that were produced by the members and consciously to inform the parallel consultation.

The history of the consultation

The organization in which this consultation and matrix took place began as a family business in 1950 specializing in the manufacture of seven-inch 45-rpm records. The founder was the son of a man who had worked for and then managed the original subcontractor to Thomas Edison's record-manufacturing business. The founder's son (third generation) bought the business from his father in 1960. The Company experienced significant expansion with the growth and popularity of long-playing (LP) records and cassettes.

In 1977, Elvis Presley's death caused a major shortfall in worldwide LP and cassette manufacturing capacity. The Company had difficulty finding investment to fund its expansion to meet demand. In addition, record labels became frantic about their inability to serve the surge in the market. The Music Division (Parent) of an entertainment media company purchased this Company in 1978 but left it not integrated; the Company's name was not changed to reflect that of the Parent until 1996, and the Parent rarely intervened in the management of the firm. With the capital resources available to them from the Parent and the onset of the next generation of media boom experienced in compact discs (CDs), the Company grew to become one of the largest providers of entertainment media in the world. In 1996, the Company produced between 400 and 500 million CDs and has contributed to the development of what might be the next generation of popular media, the digital videodisc (DVD).

The evolution of a consultation

The birth of this matrix, with its subsequent consultation, is firmly planted in the work done at the WAWI programme. Maltz and a colleague met at the Organizational Development Network of Greater New York, and they decided to collaborate on the theme of how individuals resist change in organizations. From this collaboration emerged a series of public and private (internal to specific organizations) workshops on "Managing Resistance to Change" (MRC: Basler & Maltz, 1997). The workshops used open systems, psychoanalytic, and group relation theory to expand personal competencies in managing oneself in role. The first of these two-day workshops, held in October 1993, was public. Attending this workshop were four senior managers (three men and a woman) from the client organization whose roles were continuous improvement (one male and the female), training, and digital process engineering. Their experience in the workshop was dramatic.

The client subsequently sent four members to each of the next two public workshops (November and December 1993)—an indication to the consultants that some dilemma existed on a relatively broad basis within the client system. From March through December 1994, ten workshops were held within the system and conducted by the consulting team of Maltz and two other consultants. CM participated in the workshop on May 20 1994.

In June 1994, a management consulting firm (MC) with expertise in the redesign of manufacturing processes was hired by the Parent Company to analyse the Music Division's supply chain— the Company's work processes through which product was made, distributed, and sold. During the late summer and autumn workshops, the anxiety and tension in the MRC workshops became extremely heightened, and the system experienced an increasing amount of violence. For example, one female manager reported being attacked and sexually harassed by a subordinate; a male manager was fired for inappropriate, sexually explicit comments during a Company dinner; numerous physical fights erupted on the shop floor; hostile graffiti in the plant increased; talk of forming a union began (this was and remains a non-union organization); job satisfaction and morale began to dive; and so on. In addition, MC, cellular manufacturing, and "sister" organizations within the Parent were all experienced by the organization's members as disruptive, unnecessary, and imposed evils. The organization was very profitable, due to internal subsidies garnered from internal pricing of finished goods, and did not see a compelling reason to change its work processes. The workshops were experienced by the executives of the firm as increasingly risky and doing something to the Company.

In October 1994, a large team of MC consultants arrived at the organization's two plants to begin the work of studying and then re-engineering the workplace. The presenting problem of this consultation was cost. The Company was producing the product at about 20¢ more than the competition and experienced numerous delays and disruptions in its delivery to its three main customers, the largest of which was the Parent's distribution company.

The MCs uncovered waste in the Company's manufacturing processes and recommended a significant change in the way that the shop floor was organized and staffed, inventory was managed, and so on. The production process was to be re-engineered from one of "batch-line" manufacturing, in which work was segmented into separate tasks on separate machines in different parts (physical and departmental) of the organization, to one of "cellular" manufacturing, in which work processes and tasks are integrated into a unit (a "cell") in a single place in the plant with a specific, role-assigned team of workers. The effort was to produce a stream-lined process, lower cost, improved customer response time and service, and preserve jobs.

On 30 November 1994, the MRC Team was asked to meet with the Company's "Quality Council" (a subgroup of the Executive Team) to discuss MRC and what was being learned. The MRC Team was experienced as ineffectual by the employees, and by certain Executive Team members. This Team was consulted to over a period of two years by the other team, MC, which consisted of three consultants (two women and a man). Over the year that the MRC Team was in the system, they made numerous attempts to meet with the MC consultants but were considered competitive and ignored. The last intervention by this other consulting team was in the spring of 1995.

This happened simultaneously with some of the violent events in the system being uncovered in the data and work of the workshop. This meeting led to the Executive Team's attendance at a special session of MRC (December 1994). During another MRC session later that month, the Vice President of Human Resources decided to stop the MRC work and end the consultation. A combination of the connection formed between the Consulting Team and the CEO during the special MRC session and the outcry from the workforce for the MRC workshops to be continued led to the Consulting Team's being re-hired in February 1995. It was clear from these events that authority was neither delegated nor clearly understood nor aligned in any productive manner.

A consultation emerges

Being fired and then re-hired offered an opportunity to expand the work of the consultation and put to use the systemic learning of the MRC workshops and the consultants' experiences. Maltz renegotiated the contract and began consulting to the system in addition to the MRC work.

The re-contracting for the MRC workshops included an attempt to bring it in-house and have the consultant team train internal workshop facilitators and the expansion of the workshop to include "large group/small group" learning. The redesign achieved a greater throughput of employees (45) and the ability to increase learning by holding three simultaneous workshops with events that brought the whole group together at specific times. Five workshops of this design were held between May and August 1955.

The facilitation of MRC began by sharing and associating to their dreams on a daily basis. This dream-work helped to unearth and process anxieties and dilemmas held by the facilitators and vastly improved their ability to work as containers for the workshop.

In March 1995, Maltz and the lead consultant from MC met and found the consultations to be compatible and helpful to one another. Between May and June 1995, the MC consultant and Maltz met periodically, and Maltz began consulting to organizational issues being raised by MC's restructuring intervention. In July 1995, the CEO asked to meet with both Maltz and the MC consultant to seek help on how to work with the intense resistance he experienced. From this conversation, a change-management team was formed that included the CEO, the MC consultant, the General Counsel/Vice President of the Parent, an additional Vice President from the Parent who was responsible for ensuring that product orders from the Music Division were properly placed and fulfilled (essentially, the key "client contact"), and Maltz.

This "Leadership Team" worked to define specific expectations of the organization's change, a methodology for that change, and a design for change leadership. A "Transition Plan" for the organization, which detailed the technical, organizational, and managerial issues and key recommendations for how the system could complete its change-over to cellular manufacturing, was agreed to in September and published to the Leadership Team in early October.

Concurrent with this process, CM and Maltz began another consulting intervention to help clarify the nature of role among "cell" team members, management, and support functions. CM and Maltz used Responsibility Charting as an intervention to help the system understand the complication of role that led to the realignment of many functions. In addition, some of the unspoken and dynamic projections onto terminology, as well as the differences in how one defined terms, were unearthed. For instance, the term "empowerment", which was used extensively by both management and the workforce, did not mean that a cell team was free to decide to change the time boundaries of a shift or even shift breaks (which was attempted). Empowerment was redefined in this system as a set of work-tasks for which one was accountable and responsible. The extent to which one was authorized in these tasks was the sum of her or his role accountability and authority; the cell team's authority was the result of what was negotiated in these systems-of-task with management.

Creating a transition space

In October 1995, the work outlined in the Transition Plan began. The three key issues of this plan (all having to do with the enormity of the task of restructuring this work-system) were:

1. That the current Executive Team could not manage the transition—a new team had to be formed. Maltz designed a process for the assessment and selection of a new Executive Team. Four managers would be selected in this process, one to manage each part of the change effort (see point 2).

2. That the organization-as-a-whole could not manage the change to cellular manufacturing while maintaining the current business. Parts of the organization needed to be bounded and focused on their specific set of challenges. One part of the system had to focus on the current batch operations (the Old), another on implementing cellular operations (the New), and a third had to help the batch transition to cellular ("transition"). In addition, finance and administration would still be required as a central resource.

3. That the CEO could not manage this change effort alone, and the Leadership Team became the operating management committee for the system's change.

On 21 October 1995, an assessment of the organization's current executives was initiated. This was the first action that symbolized a permanent change to the existing management (though the formation of the Leadership Team sent a powerful prior signal to the organization).

In November 1995, another colleague (James Krantz of Triad Consulting Group LLC) joined Maltz specifically to work with the Transition Team. Additionally, Walker was hired by Maltz to "shadow" him during a day of consultation in the system in order to help Maltz work with his conscious and unconscious processes. November was also the month in which the matrix began, the events of which are described in the next section.

Consulting to change

In December 1995, the CEO negotiated his retirement with the Parent; he would stay on in various roles for another six months. The new CEO was well known to the system and considered by many, in their experience, to be a cause of problems for them both in his apparent lack of support for cellular manufacturing and in his organization's response as a member of the supply chain. It is unclear where these experiences were derived from. The new CEO certainly represented much to this organization in reality and symbolically. This included the "take-over" by the Parent, the end of the "family" business, the end of their "freedom", the first non-region/non-family "boss" (a New Yorker), their ambivalence about the change and the consultation by MC, and so on.

In February, the Management Team began grappling with the issues in front of them and soon discovered that costs in the system remained significantly above that of the competition. Decreasing the number of employees became therefore an obvious and necessary part of the strategy for change.

On 14 March 1996, the first ever voluntary retirement programme was announced by the Management Team. The goal was to "retire" approximately 100 employees with extensive length of service (some back to 1960). The programme was a success.

MC, having completed their assignment, handed over the manufacturing consultation to the organization in April 1996. Less than one-third of the organization had undergone the transition to cellular manufacturing at this time, but the "experiment" of cellular operations seemed to prove sound, and plans were finalized to move the rest of the organization aggressively by January 1997. A softening in the music industry together with changes in the Parent's Parent and capital expense/investment issues were part of this decision.

In June 1996, a number of significant events occurred: the former CEO retired officially; the organization's name was changed to that of the Parent; a new internal operating structure, which focused on cellular manufacturing plants, each responsible for a different customer segment, was developed; and the decision was made to reduce the number of employees by about 20%. Between 26 June and 2 July 1996, the system reduced the workforce by approximately 400 people. Triad consulted to this downsizing.

In early July, a member of the Management Team accused Maltz of breaking confidentiality about what was discussed in the Management Team with members of the organization and specifically with CM. Confidentiality had long been an issue in this system. It seemed that as soon as executives made any decision, the organization knew about it. Information was continually being leaked by most of the members of the Management Team to their confidants within the system.

Triad Consulting decided to discontinue its participation in the matrix as part of the process of "securing" the boundary around the work being done with the Management Team. On 14 July 1996, the matrix was ended. Triad's contract with and, thus, consultancy to this system ended in January 1997.

Significant events
of this applied social dreaming matrix

The matrix

As mentioned above, the dream matrix began in November 1995. Until its end in July 1996, it accumulated 122 dreams and associations from the client system, the external consultant (Maltz), and the dream consultant (Walker). The 48 contributions from CM included dreams by five other members of the client system, indicating that the matrix was "pulling" dreams from different parts of the client system. Maltz and Walker made 36 and 38 contributions, respectively. Figure 2 shows the frequency of contributions by month against the total consultation to this system (the consultation began in October 1993 and ended in January 1997). As can be seen from Figure 3, the life cycle of the matrix can be divided into a beginning, a middle, and an end, each lasting three months. In order to report most efficiently on the content of the matrix, these distinct phases are described individually here, and examples are provided of dreams containing key issues corresponding to each phase.

The beginning

As was noted earlier, this on-line matrix grew out of a dream and an association to that dream. The dream occurred to Walker in September 1995 and was shared on-line with CM by Maltz. The dream was about *a scientific presentation in New York by a psychoanalytic organizational consultant, which had been proclaimed as the "be all to end all" paper for laying out a unified field theory for socioanalysis by introducing a "third force" between sentience and task. Subsequent to the presentation, which was attended by the entire socio-analytic community, Walker and Maltz accompanied the presenter to his apartment to get ready for a reception to recognize this great achievement. At the apartment, his enormous wife—who furiously lambasted him on being a useless, ineffectual person, especially around the house—accosted the presenter. Listening to her made Walker and Maltz and the presenter late for the reception. The three of them then took a subway to the wrong subway station, very far away.*

CM's desire to share her associations to this dream grew out of the parallels between it and her recent experiences at work around Maltz's consultation. She noted that this dream paralleled her fantasy of accompanying a co-worker to New York to meet a new organizational consultant to the client system, about whom she had a "preconceived respect", to learn about action research. The presenter in the dream being "put down" by his wife reminded

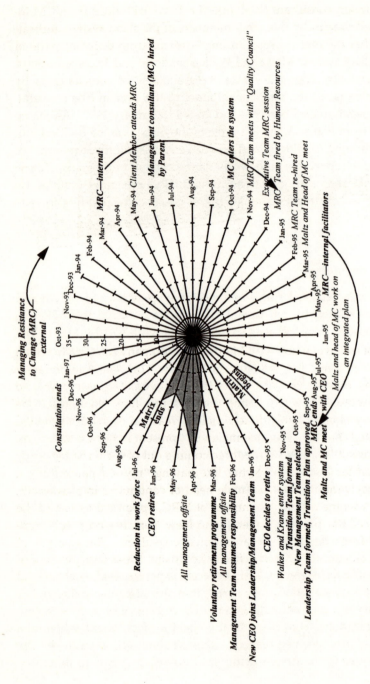

Figure 2: *History of the Consultation and Frequency of Participant Dream and Association Submissions*

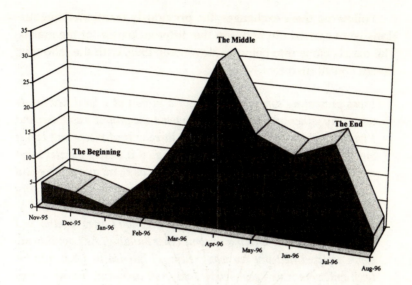

FIGURE 3: Frequency of Dreams

her of a conversation with Maltz in the company cafeteria in which she mentioned her desire to go to New York and subsequently feeling that Maltz had doubts that she would have anything to contribute. The wife's telling the presenter how "ineffectual" he was symbolized how much Maltz's reaction had hurt her. She equated it to the "punitive maleness" present in her work system. The dream's end, with the three coming out of the wrong subway station far away, was to her like having "my ass parked in ... Pennsylvania, while MA [male head of continuous improvement, who was the original champion of MRC, appointed as one of the first cellular plant managers] is in New York meeting and learning" from this new organizational consultant. This sample of associations, which arose from the dream, illustrates the experience so often noted in the matrix—dreams that validate, label, and freely express feelings that are otherwise unavailable when consulting to a system or, more so, when working as part of a system. It was the strength of this client's experience, as expressed through the lucidity of her associations, which brought the matrix into being.

Following these exchanges, the previously mentioned negotiations were carried out between the different parties of the matrix. The matrix came into being in November 1995, with the following dream contributed by CM:

I was presenting some work I did for a project at a local newspaper where my father works. I don't know what the project was about, but I had brought it to the newspaper in three curved pieces and laid it out for all to see. The pieces fit together as if it were a puzzle. I was explaining that I was not finished with it, as there was a piece still missing. The audience (of which my father was a member) was very pleased with what I had done so far. They told me they would be excited to see the finished product. I gathered my things together as I had to go to another meeting in some other building. As I got into my car, I realized that my key was melting. I hurried to get it into the ignition before it was completely limp. As I turned it, the car started and at the same time an acid-like substance began spraying out of my dashboard through the vents. It was burning my skin so I got out of the car . . . which began rolling backwards. I opened the door and stuck my foot in . . . to put the brakes on. I could not take my foot off the brake . . . for fear that the car would hit the red truck behind me. I knew the truck belonged to _____ [a male colleague] and I knew he was just in the same meeting I came from, so I just waited for him. Some of the other men that were at the meeting began to walk by, including my father. They looked and saw what was happening, but none stopped to help me. My father just yelled at me that I didn't need to keep my foot on the brake because the car wasn't running. But I knew it was. I was very angry that no one was helping me as I stood there, half in and half out of the car . . . this is when I woke up.

The parallels in the first part of the dream are to the business (media), the father (CEO), and to the three-part model for organizational transition which had just been created by the consultancy. Less obvious is the mention of a missing piece in the three-part design, which refers to the then lack of a new management team subsequently formed in the month following this dream.

In addition to the parallels to the structural elements of the system seen above, the dream's melting key, spraying acid, and impending car accident provide images of failure and injury. At the outset of the matrix, it was unclear as to whether these predict subsequent events in the consultation around the downsizing of the company or simply reflect the visceral experience of being a member of this system. In any case, the juxtaposition of recognition for achievements and impending disaster, which appear in the beginning phase of the matrix, continued in the second dream and throughout the matrix. WA (young female, cellular process coach) offered this dream:

I was alone sleeping in my new house, and there was a black snake in each of the two bedrooms. I knew one snake was poisonous and one was not . . . and I tried to be careful when I walked through the doorway. Then I was at an Army training school, and MB [young ambitious male with a background in finance, appointed as the second cellular plant manager] was the area manager, and he wore a red shirt. We were in a classroom sitting at desks . . . there was a girl behind me who was just like me. MB said hello to me but . . . went to the other girl to ask her opinion on something, and I could tell he had a lot more respect for her. Later, walking next to a pond, . . . I passed WB [middle-aged female pre-press operator] talking to a man with a beard . . . standing by an old red truck talking about work. . . . I then came upon a deer that had been hit by a car . . . lying on its side. . . . I could tell it was in a lot of pain and was waiting for someone to help. It started to sit up; it slid out onto the road and another car came along and ran over its leg. Then it slid some more, and I was afraid it would slide into the pond and drown. I ran over and held its head in my arms, and there was a lot of blood. I yelled to the man with the beard to help me, because drowning like that would be a horrible death. He and WB came over, and the man said: "You know its going to die, right?" I said: "Yes but couldn't we slit it's throat so it would just go to sleep instead of drowning?" The man with the beard said he would like to keep the deer skin, so he couldn't slit its throat because it would ruin it. I said "OK", and then cut its femoral artery. . . . After cutting the skin, they slowly lifted the hipbone out of the skin but the deer didn't bleed. So, they . . . kept cutting it trying to make it bleed . . . the deer . . . looked at me and seemed a little stronger. Then I saw the missing leg and where the empty skin was hanging down with blood on the edges, and I got such a sick feeling in my stomach. I thought we did this to its leg, but WHAT IF? What if the deer could be saved?

All in all, there were eight offerings during the first three months of the matrix, five of which were dreams and the rest associations. The final dream of this phase was from WC (young Jewish female, newest member of the continuous improvement staff). It described *the dilemma of talking to a friend of hers about going for a PhD in I/O Psychology. The friend pleaded with her not to, because the head of the I/O programme was a consulting client and she was afraid of losing confidentiality.* This particular dream was only associated to by CM and was difficult to place in the context of the matrix, until the planning of a presentation related to the consultation and the matrix. At that point, the writer faced a similar conflict because they wanted CM to participate in the presentation panel, recognizing her authority in role to communicate this; however, she was not permitted to be involved in any way, in case the system's identity was revealed.

The middle

The middle phase took place between February and April 1996. This phase was punctuated by an enormous burst of activity (see Figures 2 and 3), consisting of seventeen offerings, which took place in the two weeks prior to the company's announcement on 14 March of its voluntary retirement programme, a prelude to substantial layoffs to come. These seventeen offerings seemed to contain many of the themes appearing throughout the matrix. The first of these dreams came to MD (young male, a member of the original cellular designs team, now a member of a cell).

> *I came out of my house, and at the bottom of my porch were ME [vice president of the "old", residual batch operations] and MF [young male manager of batch operations, reporting to ME]. They were looking at the cells and asking me how the other Area was doing. I went around to the back of my house, which is where the other Area was supposed to be. However, when I got there I looked down at the cells and realized they were only little sprouts . . . that had not been growing. I looked closer at them to see if I could see any numbers on them but I could not. I ran into my house and pulled out some binders to see if I could find the production figures but took . . . a long time and*

began to panic, thinking that if I can't give them these figures . . . I was going to lose my job. By the time I had come back out to the front of the house . . . I saw that they were gone. Later that night (still in the dream) I saw the two of them at a bar and they barely said Hi to me. I thought I was going to be fired.

Embedded in the technical issues of the re-engineering of the manufacturing process presented by this dream are powerful psychological themes that are repeated throughout the matrix. In this dream, the entire re-engineering process is cast as a drama enacted between the "sprouts" as a symbol of failed regeneration (the need to "get numbers" to satisfy the bosses) and the fear of being fired. Hence, the images of destruction and persecution heavily outweigh the images of regeneration and growth. CM describes it as a battle between the batch and cell managers at a time when the batch managers were regrouping within the company and "resurfacing" to recoup some of their lost influence. In fact, the batch vice president (ME), whose future career had been in question during this transformation, later became the vice president of the catalogue and mail order divisions created out of the transition itself.

In Maltz's dream subsequent to this, *he was in an office that had a front door and no walls, as if on a cloud where only the floor was solid. He was verbally sparring with a "brash young type . . . dressed in a blue double-breasted suit with a white shirt with stripes". Another man who was intimidated by him also accompanied this individual.* Here, the contrast of the New and the Old continues via images of the "dressed-down" process consultant in an open-space office sparring with the traditionally dressed businessman who is experienced as persecutory by his presumably subordinated associate. As is often the case in social dreaming, CM's associations grew out of the seemingly insignificant fact of the suit being blue and the shirt being white. She wrote:

"This can apply to . . . the dilemmas of the blue-/white-collar workers at our plant. Being a 'blue-collar' worker now has become the safest of positions in the ever-changing and increasingly flattening organization. The over-layers of management [are] now facing the realization that they must now take on roles that may have appeared beneath them. . . . The lack of walls . . . seems to reflect the organization that we are painstakingly trying to create . . . with boundaries that are . . . spoken to and clarified. [However,] the cloud-like feeling [reflects] the state that the company is in at present [where] . . . no one is sure of the ground they stand on."

Simultaneously with Maltz's dream of the blue-suited businessman, Walker had a dream in which

he arrived at a friend's house in Chicago, which turned out to be empty. A pushcart went by, laden with delicious cakes being peddled by a tall white man with dark hair. Later, two women arrived whispering to each other, and one of them had marks on her face that were clearly the result of a beating. She said that her boyfriend had hit her in the face, and she went on whispering with her friend about how to pay the peddler, who actually was a gangster hit-man, to exact revenge for the beatings which she had endured for too long. After they arranged the hit, Walker told them that murder was out of proportion to the beatings and that they would be caught and sent to jail for life. They panicked and ran off to try to reverse the hit but were too late. Meanwhile, a male inhabitant of the house arrived and insisted that the hit was perfectly normal.

This dream was followed by an association from Maltz that he was the hit-man. After this, he offered the following dream:

I am with friends, two men and a woman. We are going to or by the woman's home. A vengeful killer is after us (or her). We are frantic, running for places to hide. One of the male friends is killed or shot and wounded seriously. I hide outside, underneath stairs that are at the front of the house, and then in the back. The killer runs by, and I go into the house looking for the others. I think the woman is with me or near me . . . but the electricity is off. I find one male friend, and we begin our search for others, not knowing where the killer is.

CM then associated this dream to the fact that she was told by a colleague that she should stay away from MA because they believed that he was "out to get her".

The following night, Maltz reported a dream that he felt should be entitled: "Build the Better Battery" or "The Pizza Method of Battery Making".

I was building or inventing batteries with mixed components, a little of this and a little of that. At one point I took a little lithium and a little of something else to develop a battery. Making the batteries included some baking (like pizza). At one point I tested the battery, which was in the shape of a long toy train that ran wonderfully around the floor of a mall-like place.

He reported feeling overjoyed at the conclusion of the dream. His first association was to the idea of bomb-making and a recent bombing in Israel that had taken place at a mall. When CM associated to this dream, she saw it as representing Maltz's attempts to "build future leaders" within the client system and that the train may be her. By linking together in time this particular subset of a dream and the three associations, the matrix had offered its first prediction that Maltz's relationship to CM would become toxic for the client–consultancy system, to the point of causing the demise of the matrix. Predicting dilemmas that were soon to come, a set of associations were offered which included the suggestion that the role, task, and authority boundaries of the matrix should be re-negotiated because of "the current manifestations of Krantz in this Matrix . . . and the fact that he is all over it but oddly inaccessible". In fact, one week later the matrix almost unravelled because CM thought that Walker was on-line with Maltz without "cc'ing" her. She threatened to boycott the matrix. In the subsequent confusion, Walker made the "mistake" of "cc'ing" a note to CM acknowledging personal and confidential information given to him by Maltz. These events drove home the fragility of this applied matrix and led the writers to realize the need to develop a greater ability to take in the consultations that the matrix itself offers concerning its own management. This set of associations concluded with an account Walker had heard that day about a Jewish "commando" who was on "staff" at Auschwitz. The commando described how the incoming masses, after being stripped and shorn, begged to be told the "truth" of what was to come of them in the showers and how the staff was told it was essential that the prisoners not be told for fear of creating "panic".

As it turned out, during the above-mentioned hiatus, CM had held back a dream that she had had the same night as Maltz's "battery-making" dream. In her dream, CM was

admitted to a hospital to have a baby. The hospital was a campus with two buildings, one for females and one for males. Maltz was in the hospital, but women were not allowed in the men's "dorm", so she went outside hoping he might see her and come out, but he didn't. As she was about to have the baby, a nurse came into her room and, upon hearing of the terrible back pain that CM was experiencing, stuck a needle in her back and began drawing a tremendous amount of blood, spilling it into a bucket. CM told the nurse that she would not be able to coagulate if she took any more. After the nurse left, MA came in and tried to have sex with her. She told him to leave and that Maltz was going to be visiting her. She had a baby boy but did not get to see him. The phone rang, and MG [a young male, creative computer programmer who was being under-utilized by the Company] congratulated her and said that he was on his way to visit. Instead, her mother and father showed up with the baby, which looked 8 months old. Since the nursery had asked, she decided to call him "MI", the name of another young male in the client system who was waiting to be utilized in one of the cellular plants being developed.

The dream immediately following CM's was the final one of this burst of activity prior to the announcement of the company's voluntary retirement programme and occurred one month before the Company's first downsizing. In the dream, Walker described his being asked to consult by a female CEO of a client that he had previously visited with Maltz:

I hesitated to take on this job because I knew Maltz was still somewhere in the system but the woman said she needed some work from me right away. After agreeing to do it, I arrived on site to consult to a meeting that the CEO was having with a group of middle managers, in which she laid out the latest plan for a reorganization which involved getting rid of one or more of the members of the team. The task of the meeting was for the group to decide . . . who should go. The anxiety in the group sky-rocketed. . . . They took a break during which the CEO asked me what she should do next. I lamely suggested a go-around, having no idea what to do, but she said, "We've already tried that". I then suggested an "Agazarian analysis" of the subgroups, inviting them to self-form and each present a separate opinion as to how to proceed, which . . . went very well. The CEO was satisfied that the problem had been solved, so I began wondering where Maltz was in the system. . . . When I found him, Maltz was angry and hurt that I had entered the system without talking to him. After this, I found myself in a taxi going to meet with the CEO, but I could not remember her name. The cab driver, who turned out to be one of the middle managers, told me her name. When I found Maltz again . . . I told him I had discovered red, sinewy globs of matter enclosed in rounded wire cages in different parts of the organization, but he was still really upset. His pain and anger put him beyond listening. I massaged his back and discovered that these blobs were also miniaturized bundles of chronic tension all over his body, so I kept working at working them out. At the meeting with the CEO, I suddenly found that her organization had changed to the Department of Juvenile Justice in charge of incarcerating adolescents awaiting trial, and that she had decided to contract with a community-based hospital, where I worked, for medical services. Later, when I asked for a description of the medical service . . . being contracted out to my hospital, she said that it was to carry out the recently enacted death penalty for the State of New York.

The end

The final phase of the matrix was between May and July 1996 and consisted of 54 dreams and associations. As noted earlier, the matrix came to an end because of anxiety in the management team that their confidentiality was being compromised. CM had the matrix's final dream on July 30, after Maltz informed us that he was withdrawing from the matrix.

I was making plans to meet MJ [the son of the retired CEO and vice president of DVD and CD-ROM production], MA, MB, WC, and some others for a get-together after work. I had to go home first and then found it was my mother's house. She was in a bedroom cleaning or folding laundry. She fumed at me and told me she wanted me out of the house and that I couldn't come back. I slumped down in a chair and began crying hysterically, asking, "Why can't you love me?" She didn't answer, and I got up, still crying, and began to help her clean, thinking this would make her love me. She said nothing, and left the room. I was crushed at her lack of response. I looked down at the floor

and realized I was in my baby's room and the rug was pulled up.
There was a thick layer of dust on the wood floor, and I began to clean
it up. Then, I ran down some steps and went outside. I saw MJ
coming up a dirt path. . . . He said to me, "We really needed you
there, CM, where the hell were you?" He was angry with me. . . . I
told him that I had a fight with my mother and that I didn't know
where everyone was meeting and that . . . was why I was late.

Learning, conclusions, and hypotheses

1. Social dreaming provides powerful confirmation of the role of
   the unconscious in organizational consultation.

2. The process that develops in response to social dreams contains
   a tension between the desire to interpret dreams and the desire
   to associate to them. The former tends to predominate in psychoanalytic communities, while the later seems more spontaneous among others. Interpretation of dreams tends to focus
   attention more on the individual, while associating to them
   enables the links between people to become elaborated. A key
   development during the WAWI study group on-line matrix
   was the debate about the difference between "interpretation"
   and "association". It seemed that the group easily moved to
   interpreting dreams as though in a therapeutic relationship, as
   opposed to associating to the dreams on the organizational or
   systemic level. This debate, and its impact on us, was significant
   in refining our ability to take the technique to the workplace.

3. Developing appropriate boundaries for a social dreaming matrix creates a unique set of dilemmas. Boundaries in organizations usually function between those that contain anxiety and
   stifle creativity and communications and, more appropriately,
   those that typically result from negotiations between sentience
   and task. Since it is difficult to separate out sentience and task
   in the functioning of the matrix itself, it does not seem possible
   to create dream matrices in the absence of boundary negotiations that relate them to a specific task. On the e-mail systems
   used by the matrix members, it was possible to identify four

functional boundaries: "to", "cc", "reply to", and "reply to all". Issues of group size and composition remain to be explored. These are complicated by, among other things, the fact that the boundary of participation in the matrix is maintained not simply by what an individual chooses to do within it but also by what the matrix itself does with both participants and non-participants in the form of dream representations.

4. The matrix often contains disowned aspects of the organization. In this case, the aspects of "feminine authority", which seem to be completely absent from the organizational system, were fully present in the matrix. This was present in the negotiation to authorize the matrix on 29 May 1995; "re: the dream matrix . . . every time I [Walker] use that word, which arose after you [Maltz] began that matrix, I associate to 'dominatrix'". The extent to which women in this particular organization could only be heard in its dreams seems significant.

5. Dream matrices may contain the creativity in an organization by institutionalizing the principle that creativity in post-industrial work organizations is expressed precisely within the individual's experience of *not* fully understanding what is going on.

6. The significance of the "on-line" nature of this consultation remains an interesting and important element that begs analysis, both from the point of view of developing a social dreaming matrix and from the opportunity for learning that arises in the parallel to the client organization's own experience. The comparison is housed in the terms "analogue" and "digital". A matrix held in a room with members present could be seen as an analogue process; dreams and associations are communicated and shared in analogue form. A matrix held on-line uses a digital process to communicate and share dreams and associations. The parallel to the client organization is in their transformation from an "old, batch-line manufacturing" or analogue process to a newer, more responsive "cellular" manufacturing or digital process. This discussion also relates to the "here-and-now" experience of what might be known as an analogue matrix versus the "processing over time" that occurs in a digital matrix. Our experience suggests that applied matrices need to be continuous (digital).

Another aspect of this discussion points to the possible benefit or, at least, juxtaposition of dreaming and associating in the digital realm—dreams and associations can be offered as they happen, instead of waiting for the physical analogue boundary of the matrix to take place. Often, those participating in this matrix woke up and entered their dream into the e-mail system, making their dream available to the matrix, regardless of whether anyone was there to read the transmission immediately. This reminds us of the process that Lawrence notes about how, in many societies (i.e. Native American), dreams and their associations are present in the organization and merely "caught" by the dreamer.

7. The need for the role of a matrix consultant became ever more apparent during the course of this work. Someone managing and consulting to the boundaries of a matrix was critical for the matrix to function. The consultant in this role performs much as one does within an organization, creating a safe place to work—in the case of a matrix, to dream and to associate.

8. Responses to the knowledge of the matrix's existence by others in the client system suggested that they felt that the existence of the matrix was doing something "toxic" to them. The matrix is fantasized as being persecutory because of its unknown-ness.

9. Dream-task definition on the entry boundary is critical for differentiating a technique for carrying it out.

10. Role, task, and authority structures have an impact on the "flow" of dreams. Role and task definitions at the outset of a digital dream matrix seem to follow the same principles as in traditional process groups: they foster the management of boundaries.

11. The experiences felt by matrix participants of being "nourished" may be how they allow for the recovery of their sense of self, which feels threatened following the de-differentiation that is often, for some reason, experienced in organizational systems.

12. Institutionalizing "emptiness" (Armstrong, 1996)—Could the ancillary structures within the client system, which grew out of the on-line social dreaming matrix (by virtue that information

was processing continuously without a conclusion), create a framework in which people are able to tolerate the unknown and bring it into their institutional life?

13. The recording of dreams and associations in a digital (in this case, e-mail) matrix provides a written (sequential) history.

14. The writers experienced the matrix as, often, consulting to the matrix.

15. Dreams that occur and remain un-associated to may contain parts of the system that are being defended against.

CHAPTER ELEVEN

Social dreaming @ work

W. Gordon Lawrence, Marc Maltz,
and E. Martin Walker

> I regard dreams as creative and aesthetic experiences that
> depict in the form of visual metaphors the present state of our
> connection and disconnection with the world about us.
>
> Ullman, 1975, p. 9

The world in which we live

This book has traced its roots and given examples of how
social dreaming has been used around the world to make
the experience of dreaming ordinary, to make dreams part
of our conscious, waking life through their appreciation, and to
see the dream as being linked to our everyday preoccupations.
Dreams are always a visual leap into the creative, composed of
the metaphors of our daily and historical life. In their metaphoric
form, dreams remain a synthesis of our connecting and discon-
necting with the world, an assembly of our everyday activities,
dilemmas, and existential puzzles. Dreams offer a unique source of
information.

In these closing years of the millenium, we are making the transition from the *industrial* society that we have been consumed by and with throughout this century to one borne in binary codes of 1s and 0s, radically altering the societal landscape into an *information* one. Information technology presents us with an unprecedented opportunity and a need to shift dramatically and expand the way in which we view and take-up work. These information technologies have enabled us to work differently, in an "acoustic" space that offers unique differences and opportunities from the "optical" space, or Euclidean space, with which we are accustomed. Acoustic space, which first began to be mastered by the discovery of wireless waves, is the space in which thoughts and thinking can be listened for, an added dimension to the optical space of industrial society, which operates by what it "sees". The emergence of information technology has now enabled a full appreciation of A. N. Whitehead's insight, published in *Science and the Modern World* in 1925, that the "universe is pure mind"—that is, acoustic space allows us to be aware of what we "hear" of our thinking in our minds.

In acoustic, imaginal space, we find that the sources of the infinite, when combined with our evolving experiencing minds, are eroding the limits between the finite and the infinite. The infinite has neither categories nor form nor number. Bion (1965, p. 151) quotes Milton—"The rising world of waters dark and deep/ Won from the void and formless infinite"—to show the process of transformation through which infinite space passes into our finite grasp (Symington & Symington, 1996, p. 8). A good example is our rapidly changing understanding of the universe, the earth, and our biological self as compared to that at the beginning of this century.

In a very real sense, we have always known acoustic-infinite space through our dreams. Our dreaming self continually surprises our waking self with the mystery, terror, and beauty of our dreams. In the world of dream, there is very often no evidence of causality. We live in our dreams as Alice did in her *Alice in Wonderland* world. In Western society, dreams have played little or no part in the life of enterprises, though certainly being present for their birth and inspiring the breakthroughs that they produce. Yet dreams are common to every person who is part of an organization (everyone dreams approximately five times per night). It is natural to want to believe that everything that one does in the workplace is rational and directed towards a particular end, completed in the moment through some ordered process. It is our belief, however, that these actions are being rehearsed, being thought through, being fought against, and being subverted in the time of dreaming, As Unamuno points out, we may just be a dream that dreams.

As we have said, industrial society had its existence in an optical, specific world. It was grounded in the three-dimensional reality of Euclidean space and was, therefore, conducted in a specific, local environment. Cause-and-effect was imagined visually, mechanistically linked, and apprehended consciously, thus belonging to the domain of the finite. Causation was defined in discrete, specific contexts. Causation, though, can be fallacious—a product of particular ontological and epistemological assumptions—having more to do with keeping the mind free from disturbing thinking about chaos.

With the development of quantum physics, and all the associated scientific thinking since the turn of the century, this straightforward view of causation no longer fits with experience. Association has supplemented causation. Free, mental associations exist in the inner, mental life of human beings, finding resonance between phenomena in optical and acoustic space. The inner, imaginal life of the individual makes connections, finds links, and mentally associates between phenomena that exist outside the individual in external reality. The context in which business, for example, is conducted is composed of what is recognized to be in the domain of the finite and is always extending, through associations, into what has hitherto been in the realm of the infinite.

David Bohm (1980) was able to operationalize the concept that everything in the universe is part of an undivided whole by suggesting a dynamic model for relating the finite to the infinite. In this model, everything in the universe is both part of a separate *explicate* (explained) order which is simultaneously enfolded constituting an *implicate* order in which each element is internally related to the whole and, therefore, to everything else. Reality, then, is a continuum of particles and waves, not exclusively a set of isolated particles in space. The explicate order of industrial society existed in a specific environment in which everything was believed to be causally related to everything else. In time, because of quantum physics, it was found that within that order was an implicate one that has provided the basis for the information society in which we are now living. The information society emerged out of the matrix of the implicate order of industrial society yet is contained by its explicate order. Thus, our inherited assumptions are continually eroded. Whatever societal construct follows, the information one will emerge—or be wrested—from its implicate order and, in turn, be contained within its explicate order.

The explicate order of the industrial society existed in a specific, local environment that had its being in optical space, in which everything was believed to be causally related to everything else. In time, through the discoveries of the sciences, it was found that within that order was an implicate one that has provided the bases for the information society in which we are now living. This is a world of "black stuff" that is non-specific and in which events are related in a non-local fashion. Our inherited assumptions are continually being eroded.

The mechanical world-view on which industrial society was founded subverted the Judaeo–Christian view of the world, which was concerned to draw all dimensions of the individual in her or his society into one coherent whole. Acoustic space, which was symbolized through the infinite and spirituality, was not taken account of, because it had to be imagined. The mechanical world-view was concerned to understand the causal relationships between phenomena and, as such, greatly simplified reality. This world-view led to what Lawrence Cahoone (1988) calls the "three pernicious dichotomies" that have plagued the Western mind since the time of the Enlightenment. The dichotomies are the split between subject and object (mind and body, inner and outer), that between the individuals and her or his relationships, and that between the world of human culture and the world of biophysical processes (pp. 233–234). The result was that

> In the West, these dichotomies robbed our individuality of its context and landed us in the deepest isolation, leading to narcissism. We were cut off from an outer confirmation of our inner life, leading to nihilism, and denied the confirmation of our ideas, leaving us with subjectivism and relativism. Each

nourished a form of alienation and the sum total of this alienation is the curse of modernism. [Zohar, 1991, pp. 217–218]

These "splits" resulted in most human beings not being able to
imagine and think through greater coherence to the world with
their place in it. Hence, we live in a fragmented world in which
human beings exploit one another—through pollution and wars,
for instance.

Quantum mechanics has replaced mechanistic world-views
and offers a way whereby we can begin to integrate ourselves into
the world. They suggest that the mind and the body are engaged in
a mutually creative relationship that is the basis for everything
that exists: they are not separate but related within a context. It is
the mind, with its capacity for experiencing and thinking, that
brings external reality into being. This external reality is internalized by individuals, who, in turn, continue the process of bringing
more of reality from the infinite into existence; the implicate is
always in a process of being wrested from the order of the explicate. The dream plays a role here, in that it cuts through to what is
known but not thought.

In this chapter, we offer a way of using the power of this
natural force of dreams in a post-modern, post-industrial setting—
one that is emerging as a simultaneous digital age. The manager of
today is confronted simultaneously by multiple data points, some
of which are often unknown to that individual; multivariate data
are often ignored while making critical decisions and certainly
overwhelm organizational attempts at capturing and utilizing information and the potential knowledge that it represents.

Information today is a key building block of an organization's
existence—the atom to its ever-expanding and changing universe.
Yet even the atom is a summation of data—an organization, a
representation of its complex sub-parts. We believe that social
dreaming is a viable and natural tool for enabling today's organization to delve into itself and emerge with an understanding that
is uniquely telling about its life. This is the information substance
of its unknown or unstated parts, its hidden past, its undiscussed
present, and, potentially, its enigmatic future. Social dreaming is a
powerful process that is rarely used in modern society, yet it is at
the core of our rapidly transforming, digital age. Social dreaming

is a technique that is dynamic, multidimensional, omnipresent, and steeped in the collective and continuous learning of those who put it to use.

Assumptions

We have studied and experienced the difficulty of hearing the voice of the unknown and/or unspoken in today's organization and thought about how these data can be made available in a constructive form, because we are aware intuitively that these thoughts are present in an organization. The following assumptions underlie the many technical and dynamic issues present in organizations and ground the application of social dreaming in them.

1. *Organizations are simple—their parts are complex*

Organizations exemplify the theory that the whole is simpler than its parts; they are systems that contain ordered processes that operate according to predictable and discernible patterns, which are known only in part or through hindsight. An organization's complexity is derived from the manner in which its parts (its divisions, sub-divisions, teams, and individuals) are connected to one another and to the greater system that each part contacts, such as suppliers, customers, stockholders, and others who may have a stake in the existence of a firm.

The overall system appears to be rather simple in functioning, yet the sets of tasks, configurations of roles, the uses of authority, the manner of work processes, and so on are each distinct and complex. For instance, the elements of a manufacturing line in an automobile assembly plant are far more complex than the overall system of manufacturing (which is simply the importing of parts that are assembled for a car to emerge). The component-supply side itself consists of numerous individual tasks, roles, interfaces, and sub-assembly and manufacturing, for instance, that precedes the inflow of parts to the plant. A delay in any part of this feeding process could potentially disrupt the entire process, as General

Motors became aware when a brake-component supplier experienced an extended strike, resulting in the eventual shut-down of General Motors' assembly operations.

2.   Organizations are multidimensional

Organizations, we understand, mostly function in a flat dimension of dyadic form (i.e. a manager and a subordinate) or triadic form (i.e. the relationship between sales, marketing, and operations), and in any flat-dimensional interpretation one considers only the two or the three components of interaction. Triads, though, are inherently unstable, as are dyadic relationships, and organizations therefore need help in reaching multidimensional interpretations of their structure and the dynamic processes contained therein, allowing them to look at not just the surface operating processes but other dimensions that are not readily apparent—a fourth dimension that expresses what is not known. This fourth dimension, which is hidden or unknown, can be likened to a re-expression of triads in pyramidal form, in which a fourth surface is always present. Such a three-dimensional view of the triadic form enables us to look at multiple triadic relationships from varied angles, with a shifting representation of a fourth and necessary component—its base or foundation. Expressing the relatedness of sales, marketing, and operations in the open, "pyramid" form allows the exploration of whatever unifies the three—the fourth in this case might be the customer, the product, the shareholder, and so on. And as we hold the pyramid in hand and turn it from side to side, the relationships among these entities take on a new light.

3.   Organizational processes are continually in flux

Organizations are in a continual state of flux, given their ever-changing environment, product technologies, market, competitive, and operating conditions, and the state of their dynamic capital of human beings. Any attempt to cast a particular strategy, programme, process, and so forth that does not simultaneously respect the human aspect and find a means of tapping it will ultimately fail. Any operational plan, by the time it has been researched, written, presented, approved, and implemented, is out of date. An example of this is currently emerging in the world of semiconductors. Moore's Law ("The rate of microchip speed and processing throughput will double every 18 months") used to be the strategic principle that guided the entire information industry. Recent developments, however, by IBM (the use of copper as a viable conductor) and by Intel (the ability to increase dramatically the flow of the number of bits or bytes in a microchip) will offer the revolutionary ability to accelerate exponentially the rate of change and future development of microprocessors, and thus the information world.

4. *Work is the container, and the organization the contained*

In the past, organizations strove to define what work was, how it was structured, and how the necessary thinking processes functioned. In today's organization, data about work and how it is enacted are available at the task level, as is the authority to effect work, which is also moving to the task-responsible and -accountable person. These result in work itself becoming the defining element, thus containing the purpose and functioning of an organization. In any successful organization today, the individual employee has become unique, trained with specific skills and vested with an authority to make critical decisions on her or his work. Organizations have imparted to their members a unique power and responsibility, vesting each with unprecedented information and control about the whole. Each position, task, and other definition of work increasingly holds and "contains" major elements of the organization-as-a-whole.

5. *Solutions are temporary*

Solutions derived from problem-solving techniques are binary and thus usually consider a finite set of data, which can only produce a finite set of answers. In the example cited in assumption 3, a plan is developed on the basis of technically outdated data sets involving events that have already occurred and may no longer be relevant by the time the plan is enacted. Problem solving—whether the modern spiral process of rapid software development, pattern/system analysis derived from and used in modern financial markets, or the more routine analysis–solution–implementation processes used everywhere—is in every case based, for the most part, on what is already known or has been published somewhere. There does not exist, though, much more known material to be tapped that might lead to alternative answers. However, when Shell Petroleum decided to look at different scenarios in the early 1970s to explore the possibility of more costly oil, this resulted in their being prepared for the 1973 oil crisis; and the use of derivatives in the late 1980s as a hedge against investment losses led to enormous new financial markets and wealth. The idea that a loosely formed network of computers, the Internet, might revolutionize communications gave rise to entire new businesses such as Netscape (within three years). These examples tell us that alternative ways of looking at existing data will lead to the discovery of unprecedented solutions.

6.   *There are no repeatable processes*

Organizations are always in the state of becoming or transforming (regardless of action), as are the processes that underlie them. When organizations are faced with challenges from the environment and its management system does not respond, or does not know how to respond, the organization suffers some level of disruption and, perhaps, bankruptcy and dissipation. Organizations that are flexible in how they exercise the rules of work-tasks and authority allow for continual flux in their processes and for daily adaptation to the critical factors of their success. Efforts to improve the efficiency of repeatable (and unrepeatable) processes that have been in vogue in recent years are actually looking to redefine the nature of work within a system under the guise of restructuring the organization. For true work design to be effective and sustainable, organizations must consider not only the known interaction between functions and the data that they produce, but the extended information "system" that contains the dynamic life of the processes and all that is readily known about them.

7.   *Organizations are simultaneously creative and destructive*

Creativity is a fundamental asset of any organization. When people within an organization tap their creativity, the enterprise has a greater potential to survive and prosper and fulfill its potential. Creativity, though, is difficult to unleash within an organization, because it is always linked to an inherent destructiveness. A creative idea always subverts the existing meaning. An idea that solves a problem, and may even lead to a breakthrough, must change something within an organization, whether a process, people, product, and so on, thus "destroying" what previously existed. The people in an organization need to find limits between creativity and destructiveness in order to manage the anxious, competitive edge that is defined by the political and other dynamic forces unleashed during the change. Those companies that have made the balance of these forces a part of their operating routine reap the benefits, such as 3M's continued success with innovative applications of their basic core strength. At 3M, an engineer's dream or thought is respected and supported—just imagine an organization without Post-it notes.

8. *Organizations are overwhelmed by information*

The rapid rate of growth of information technology has dramatically shifted the nature of knowledge within organizations and has enabled access to what was in the domain of the infinite (for the technical reality of this, refer to the earlier mention of Moore's Law). Currently, the entry of tremendous volumes of information into the domain of finite structures leaves organizations overwhelmed. Current attempts at cataloguing, understanding, and managing this data, such as "knowledge management", bring their importance to the forefront yet offer limited success because they do not consider all of an organization's information, only that which is readily available in existing databases. Few, if any, organizations consider the information contained in the unspoken thoughts of their employees, and to do so would create a further deluge which cannot be absorbed in an already inadequate information infrastructure.

9. *An organization's thinking is its key asset*

Knowledge is arrived at through the process of thinking about the meaning of information—a process of revelation. An organization is fuelled foremost by the nature of its thinking as opposed to any other factor. Exploration of an organization's vast volume of thinking—critical for an organization to understand emergent information and then allow the results to materialize—is difficult, again, because of its destructive nature. Organizations need a means to tap their thinking and harness their greatest asset.

Social dreaming
and the unthought known in organizations

Given the reality of organizations today, as represented in these nine assumptions, a new approach to organizational data that also allows for creative thinking and synchroneity is clearly needed. We believe that symbiont techniques, such as social dreaming, are necessary for accessing the fourth dimension in organizational work—that information that is either unspoken or not yet known— thus expanding the availability of critical information to a system. "Symbiont" denotes the smaller of two entities linked in symbiosis: the "mutual cooperation between persons and groups in society" (*Webster's Dictionary*). The nature of collaboration between persons and groups in organizations must include systematic processes for accessing the unknown and the "unthought known", as well as the humility to recognize that what is known will always be less than the data sets available at any given moment.

As we have demonstrated, organizations are essentially not what we think they appear to be, particularly so when we are trying to understand them in the context of the information society. There is always an implicate order present in the explicate order with which we try to deal. Much of our understanding of organizations derives from a stream of thought that has its roots in the mechanistic world-view, which deals with the explicate order. Little, if any, attention is paid to the complexities of the mind. What theorists tend to see is that man is rational, and they consistently work on this assumption by reducing all complexity to the explicate, the easily understandable.

A dream is a representation of the reality of a dreamer within a context that is arrived at through the work of the brain during sleep, which creates the possibility of both imagination and self-understanding (Hobson, 1988). It is the dream that links the human being to the rational world of the organization. Therapeutically and interpersonally, dreams have been interpreted as being the personal property of the dreamer. Yet, as the chapters in this book have demonstrated, there is ample evidence that dreams are not solely the property of the dreamer but belong to the greater context of which the dreamer is a part—the place that the dreamer holds in her or his daily life and personal and work roles.

Dreams have their seeds in the world. Social reality is the context in which dreams have their bases. Dreams, through their metaphors, provide us with the feelings that connect, or disconnect, us to our society. They are creative syntheses, if we could only appreciate them.

Dreams arise from the black hole of the psyche, which contains an enormous amount of condensed material of all our experiences that falls outside the realm of our consciousness (Ullman, 1975). This condensed material transcends time and space. We dream, and in that process we usher ourselves into the realm of this condensed material, which is experienced non-verbally. The dream makes us expand the condensed material and unfold it, making what is implicate become explicate—that is, disentangling what is enfolded in the dream. When we reach the waking state, a second transformation occurs in that the implicate contained in the explicate of the dream is verbalized. We put the dream into words in order to tell it to another. "What is implicate at one stage becomes explicate in the next stage through a process of unfolding, and what is explicate at this stage becomes implicate for the next stage." (Ullman, 1975, p. 9). This Ullman makes clear in a diagram (see Figure 4).

In any organization, all are connected through their role relationships—as individuals, pairs, groups, teams—yet all are also connected to one another through an organizational purpose and a matrix of connective thinking. There is always a domain of thinking that is unique to an organization and marks it off from another, as well as the thinking that informs other aspects of our world.

Through a social dreaming matrix, this thinking can be tapped into, appreciated, and understood. The black hole of the individual psyche will be reaching towards the unity that exists and which each of us intuits. Once dreams are dreamt, they may be successfully applied to a common purpose and become information for

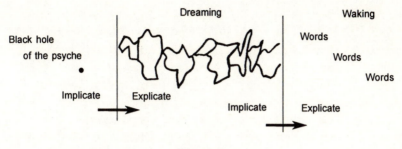

FIGURE 4

any system in which the dreamer is a member. History provides innumerable examples of innovations dreamt, the most famous being Einstein's $e = mc^2$ and Kekulé's discovery of the structure of the benzene ring after he dreamt of a snake swallowing its own tail. When the nature of the symbiont collaboration between persons and groups in organizations is expanded to include strategies for accessing the unknown (infinite)—the unthought known—the potential for creative work is expanded exponentially. An organization that can enable its dream life to emerge will be able to further the work of its parts and its whole and provide a framework for continuous learning that emerges from the system, simultaneously allowing the system to emerge.

REFERENCES

Ackoff, R. (1981). *Creating the Corporate Future*. New York: John Wiley.

Agazarian, Y. (1993). *Training Workbook: Systems-Centred Theory*. Philadelphia, PA.

Agazarian, Y. (1994). The phases of group development and the systems-centered group. In V. L. Schermer & M. Pines (Eds.), *Ring of Fire*. London: Routledge.

Allen, R. F., & Kraft, C. (1982). *The Organizational Unconscious*. Englewood Cliffs, NJ: Prentice-Hall.

Armstrong, D. G. (1992). Names, thoughts and lies: the relevance of Bion's later writing for understanding *Experiences in Groups*. *Free Associations, 3* (Part 2, No 2): 261–282.

Armstrong, D. G. (1994). *The "Unthought Known."* London: The Grubb Institute.

Armstrong, D. G. (1996). *The Recovery of Meaning*. New York: ISPSO Conference.

Baird, N. (1994). *The Dream Team Group: Members Sharing Dreams as an Organizational Development Process*. MBA Thesis, Swinburne University, Swinburne, Australia.

Bates, R. J. (1987). Corporate culture, schooling, and educational administration. *Educational Administration Quarterly, 23* (4): 79–115.

Bateson, G. (1973). *Steps to an Ecology of Mind.* St Albans: Paladin.

Basler, F., & Maltz, M. (1997). Managing resistance to change. In: A. Hiam (Ed.), *The Portable Conference on Change Management.* Amherst, MA: HRD Press.

Benton, J. (1990*). Naomi Mitchison.* London: Pandora.

Beradt, C. (1968). *The Third Reich of Dreams.* Chicago, IL: Quadrangle Books.

Bion, W. R. (1961). *Experiences in Groups.* London: Tavistock Publications.

Bion, W. R. (1965). Language and the schizoid patient. In M. Klein, P. Heimann, & E. Money-Kyrle (Eds.), *New Directions in Psycho-Analysis.* London: Tavistock Publications. [Reprinted London: Karnac Books, 1977.]

Bion, W. R. (1970). *Attention and Interpretation.* London: Tavistock Publications. [Reprinted London: Karnac Books, 1988.]

Bion, W. R. (1975). *Brazilian Lectures.* London: Karnac Books, 1990.

Bion, W. R. (1985). *All My Sins and The Other Side of Genius.* Oxford: Fleetwood Press.

Bion, W. R. (1991). *A Memoir of the Future.* London: Karnac Books.

Bion, W. R. (1992). *Cogitations.* London: Karnac Books.

Bleakley, A. (1989). *Earth's Embrace.* Bath: Gateway.

Bohm, D. (1980). *Wholeness and the Implicate Order.* London: Routledge & Kegan Paul.

Bollas, C. (1987). *The Shadow of the Object.* London: Free Association Books.

Borges, J. L. (1993). *Ficciones.* London: Everyman Library.

Braxton, E., & Klein, E. (1996). "How to apply open systems theory in work settings." Programme handout, Advanced Application Group Dynamics Training Course, Delray Beach, FL, The Midwest Centre of the A. K. Rice Institute.

Brennan, A. (1986). *Shakespeare's Dramatic Structures.* London: Routledge.

Brody, H. (1986). *Maps and Dreams.* London: Faber.

Cahoone, L. E. (1988). *The Dilemma of Modernity.* New York: State University of New York Press.

Clift, J. D., & Clift, W. B. (1988). *The Hero Journey in Dreams*. New York: Crossroads.

Cohn, R. C. (1969). From couch to circle to community. In H. Ruitenbeck (Ed.), *Group Therapy Today*. New York: Atherton Press.

Crossan, J. D. (1988). *The Dark Interval*. Sonoma, CA: Polebridge Press.

Davis, S. M. (1984). *Managing Corporate Culture*. Cambridge, MA: Ballinger.

Deal, T. E., & Kennedy, A. A. (1982). *Corporate Cultures: The Rites and Rituals of Corporate Life*. Reading, MA: Addison-Wesley.

De Mare, P., Piper, R., & Thompson, S. (1991). *Koinonia: From Hate Through Dialogue, to Culture in the Large Group*. London: Karnac Books.

Deming, W. E. (1993). *The New Economics: for Industry, Government, Education*. Cambridge, MA: MIT Center for Advanced Engineering Study.

Dyer, W. G. (1985). The cycle of cultural evolution in organizations. In R. H. Kilmann (Ed.), *Gaining Control of the Corporate Culture*. San Francisco, CA: Jossey-Bass Publishers.

Eisold, K. (1994). The intolerance of diversity in psychoanalytic institutes. *International Journal of Psychoanalysis, 75* (4): 215–233.

Freud, S. (1900). *The Interpretation of Dreams. Standard Edition*, 4.

Fromm, E. (1980). *Greatness and Limitations of Freud's Thought*. London: Cape.

Gillespie, G. (1988). When does lucid dreaming become transpersonal experience. *Psychiatry Journal University of Ottawa, 13*: 2

Gleick, J. (1987). *Chaos: Making a New Science*. New York: Viking Penguin.

Hall, E. T. (1966). *The Hidden Dimension*. New York: Anchor Books.

Hart, A. W. (1991). Leader succession and socialization: a synthesis. *Review of Educational Research, 61* (4) : 451–474.

Hirschhorn, L. (1988). *The Workplace Within: Psychodynamics of Organizational Life*. Cambridge, MA: MIT Press.

Hobson, J. A. (1988). *The Dreaming Brain*. New York: Basic Books.

Holloway, J. (1977). *The Proud Knowledge*. London: Routledge & Kegan Paul.

Jaques, E. (1951). *The Changing Culture of a Factory*. London: Tavistock Publications.

Jung, C. G. (1953). *Psychological Reflections*. Bollinger Series XXXI. New York: Panther.

Jung. C. G. (1964). *Memories, Dreams and Reflections*, recorded and edited by Amiela Jaffe. London: Collins and Routledge & Kegan Paul.

Kelly, A. (1992). Revealing Bakhtin. *New York Review of Books* (24 September), pp. 44–48.

Kets de Vries, M., & Miller, D. (1984). *The Neurotic Organization*. San Francisco, CA: Jossey-Bass.

Lasch, C. (1979). *The Culture of Narcissism*. New York: Warner Books.

Lawrence, W. G. (1979). *Exploring Individual and Organizational Boundaries*. Chichester: John Wiley.

Lawrence, W. G. (1985). Beyond the frames. In M. Pines (Ed.), *Bion and Group Psychotherapy*. London: Routledge & Kegan Paul.

Lawrence, W. G. (1989). Ventures in social dreaming. *Changes, 7*: 3.

Lawrence, W. G. (1991). Won from the void and formless infinite: experiences of social dreaming. *Free Associations, 2* (Part 2, No. 22): 254–266.

Lawrence, W. G. (1994). The politics of salvation and revelation in the practice of consultancy. In R. Casemore, G. Dyos, A. Eden, K. Kellner, J. McAuley, & S. Moss (Eds.), *What Makes Consultancy Work?* London: South Bank University Press.

Lawrence, W. G. (1995a). Totalitaere sindstilstande i institutioner. *Agrippa, 16* (1–2): 53–72.

Lawrence, W. G. (1995b). Totalitarian states of mind. *Journal of Health Care Chaplaincy, Canterbury* (October): 11–22.

Lawrence, W. G. (Ed.) (1996a). *Roots in a Northern Landscape*. Edinburgh: Scottish Cultural Press.

Lawrence, W. G. (1996b). Socialt drömmande och vardagsliv. In: S. V. Boëthius & Jern, S. (Eds.), *Den Suårfångade Organisationen* (pp. 194–215). Stockholm: Natur och Kultur.

Lawrence, W. G., Bain, A., & Gould, L. (1996). The fifth basic assumption. *Free Associations, 6* (Part 1, No. 37): 28–55.

Lawrence, W. G., & Daniel, P. (1982). *A Venture in Social Dreaming*. London: Tavistock.

Lifton, R. J. (1987). *The Future of Immortality*. New York : Basic Books.

McCulloch, W. S . (1965). *Embodiments of Mind*. Boston, MA: MIT Press.

McLuhan, M. (with Q. Fiore) (1967). *The Medium Is the Message: An Inventory of Effects*. New York: Bantam Books.

Meier, C. A. (1987). *The Meaning and Significance of Dreams*. Boston, MA: Sigo Press.

Meltzer, D. (1984). *Dream-Life*. Strathclyde: Clunie Press.

Michael, T. A. (1994). *Creating New Cultures: The Contribution of Social Dreaming. International Perspectives on Organizations in Times of Turbulence*. Swinburne: Swinburne University.

Morgan, H. (1998). Between fear and blindness—the white therapist and the black patient. *British Journal of Psychotherapists, 3* (34): 48–61.

Morgan, H. (1998). Looking for the crevices: consultations in the National Health Service. *Soundings, 8* (Spring): 171–183.

Morgan, H., & Thomas, K. (1996). A psychodynamic perspective in group processes. In: M. Wetherall (Ed.), *Identities, Groups and Social Issues*. London: Sage.

Morson, G., & Emerson, C. (1990). *Mikhail Bakhtin: Creation of a Prosaics*. Stanford, CT: Stanford University Press.

Oeser, F. (1992). *Social Dreaming and Shakespeare*. London: Sicnarf Press.

Ogawa & Asai (c. 1930). *Traditions and Myths of the Taiwan Aborigines*, extracted by R. H. Baudhuin (1960). Typescript held by Maryknoll Missionaries, Taiwan.

Olson, I. (Ed.) (1995). *No Other Place*. Edinburgh: Tuckwell Press.

Peters, T., & Waterman, R. H. (1982). *In Search of Excellence: Lessons from America's Best Run Companies*. New York: Harper & Row.

Penrose, R. (1989). *The Emperor's New Mind*. Oxford: Oxford University Press.

Progoff, I. (1975). *At a Journal Workshop*. New York: Dialogue House Library.

Radcliffe-Brown, A. R. (1922). *The Andaman Islanders*. Cambridge: Cambridge University Press, 1964.

Roberts, A., & Mountford, C. P. (1965). *The Dreamtime*. Adelaide: Rigby.

Saint-Denys, Marquis de (1867). *Les Rêves et les Moyens de les Diriger*, ed. M. Schatzman. London: Duckworth, 1982.

Savary, L. M. (1984). *Dreams and Spiritual Growth*. New York: Paulist Press.

Schein, E. H. (1985). *Organizational Culture and Leadership*. San Francisco, CA: Jossey-Bass.

Shakespeare, W. (1988). *The Complete Works*. Oxford: Oxford University Press.

Stewart, K. (1969). Dream theory in Malaya. In: C. Tait (Ed.), *Altered States of Consciousness*. Chichester: Wiley.

Storr, A. (1988). *The School of Genius*. London: Deutsch.

Summerson, J. (1949). *Heavenly Mansions and Other Essays on Architecture*. London: Cresset.

Sutton, P. (1988). *Dreamings: The Art of Aboriginal Australia*. New York: George Brazilier and the Asia Society Galleries.

Symington, J., & Symington, N. (1996). *The Clinical Thinking of Wilfred Bion*. London: Routledge.

Tannen, D. (1990). *You Just Don't Understand: Women and Men in Conversation*. New York: Ballantine Books.

Tolstoi, L. (1912). *Anna Karenina*. London: J. M. Dent

Trice, H. M., & Beyer, J. M. (1993). *The Culture of Work Organizations*. Englewood Cliffs, NJ: Prentice-Hall.

Ullman, M. (1975). The transformation process in dreams. New York: *The American Academy of Psychoanalysis*, 19 (2): 8–10.

Ullman, M. (1981). Psi communication through dream sharing. *Parapsychological Review*, 12 (2).

Ullman, M. (1989). Dreams and society. In: M. Ullman & C. Limmer (Eds.), *The Variety of Dream Experience*. Northampton: Crucible.

Unamuno, M. de (1954). *Tragic Sense of Life*. New York: Dover.

Van der Post, L. (1986). *A Walk with a White Bushman*. London: Chatto & Windus.

Weisbord, M. R. (1987). *Productive Workplaces: Managing for Dignity, Meaning, and Community*. San Francisco, CA: Jossey-Bass.

Wheatley, M. J. (1992). *Leadership and the New Science*. San Francisco, CA: Berrett-Koehler Publishers.

Wink, W. (1973). *The Bible in Human Transformation*. Philadelphia, PA: Fortress Press.

Young, R. (1994). *Mental Space*. London: Process Press.

Zohar, D. (1991). *The Quantum Self*. London: Flamingo

INDEX

Ackoff, R., 110
acoustic space, 6, 170, 171, 172
action research, 119, 125–128, 136,
        139, 143, 144, 153
    application of, to corporate
        culture, 109
    tool, social dreaming as, 52,
        123–140
Agazarian, Y., 65–67, 115
    analysis, 162
aggressor, identification with, 22
Allen, R. F., 110
Amitzi, V., 19
amplification, 1, 2, 4, 8, 125, 139
analytic psychology, application of
        social dreaming in, 69–73
Andaman Islanders, dream
        theories of, 35
Andreas-Salomé, L., 11
anxiety:
    in bureaucracy, 114
    -dreams, 38

evidence of, in dreams, 78–83,
        88, 132
    in groups, 162
    occasioned by dreams, 88
    psychotic:
        managers', 126
        in organizations, 138
    signal, 101
    students', 55, 57
Archean period, 3
Armstrong, D. G., xvii–xxi, 4, 10,
        12, 22, 34, 47, 91–106, 127,
        166
Asai, 14
association(s) to dreams, xvii, xix,
        27, 70, 72, 81
    Australian, 26
    blind architect dream, 10
    of business managers, 124,
        131–132
    as containers of meaning, 105
    and discovery of meanings, 35

association(s) to dreams (*continued*)
   as focus of social dreaming
      matrix, 17, 92, 125
   German, 24, 25
   holistic approach to, 1, 75
   inexpressible, 85
   vs. interpretation, 164
   Israeli, 21, 22, 23
   languages of, 34
   in matrix:
      morphological representation
         of, 27
      multi-verse of, 31, 137
   others', 46, 47, 52, 64
   as parable of Presbyterian
      Church, 120
   patterning of, xx
   of primitive Christians, 119
   related to reorganization of
      major manufacturer,
      141–167
   search for connections in, 70
   Senoi, 37
   simultaeous and sequential
      nature of, 144
   social content of, 18, 75
   solutions through, 37
Atman, 1
Australian Aborigine dream
      theories, 25–27
   Dreamtime, 26, 139
Australian Institute of Social
      Analysis, 27

Bain, A., 27, 124
Baird, N., 139
Bakhtin, M., 76, 86, 89
Basler, F., 146
Bates, R. J., 113
Bateson, G., 102
Beethoven, L. van, 10–12
Benton, J., 17
Beradt, C., xviii, 15–17, 24, 118

Bettelheim, B., 16
Beyer, J. M., 108
Bion, W. R., xviii, xix, 41, 53, 94,
      100, 103, 104, 109, 125
   on artificial blindness, 11
   on availability for thought, 33
   on experiences in groups, 12, 17,
      142
   on "O", 41
   on psychoanalytic theories of
      mind, 32
   on sculpture as capturing light,
      104
   on transformation from infinite
      to finite, 170
   on vertices of Oedipus and
      sphinx, 5
   on past and future, 106
   on psychotic thinking, 7
   questioning of boundaries,
      103–104
   on signal anxiety, 101
   on thought in search of thinker,
      3, 138
Biran, H., 19
Bleakley, A., 35
blindness:
   artificial, and creativity, 11
   and vision, 58
Bohm, D., xix, 171
Bollas, C., 60, 126
Borges, J. L., 8
boundary(ies):
   cosmos without, 1
   created by people, 1
   between cultural systems,
      fluidity of, 113
   dreams without, 2
   functions of, 102–106
   of mental space, xx
   between people, 29
   and systems, 102
Brahman, 1

Braxton, E., 67
Brennan, A., 81
Brigham Young University, Utah, 110
British Medical Association, 15
Brody, H., 36
Bruce, R., 118
Bruegel, P., the Elder, 34
butterfly effect, 114

Cahoone, L. E., 172
Canadian Broadcasting Corporation, 19
careers, idealization of, 124
causation, 171
censor, dream, 2, 28, 32
change:
    management of, 99–100
    vs. transformation, 98–102
chaos:
    fear of, 126
    theory, 110
Chattopadhyay, G., 1
Clift, J. D., 31
Clift, W. B., 31
Clinton, B., 111
Cohn, R. C., 143
collaboration within organizations, nature of, 179–181
communication:
    through acoustic space, 6
    increased, and increased anxiety, 69
    of thoughts, 95
concretization and dreaming, 2
condensation and dreaming, 2
consultancy tool, social dreaming as, 123–140
container:
    business as, 124
    circular seating of group as, 66
    group as, 63

for/of meaning, dream as, 105–106
    seminar as, 31
    social dreaming matrix as, xix, 71, 73
    work as, 176
corporate cultures, and shared experience of members, 107–121
corporate future, creation of, 110
countertransference, 143
    as context of dream, xxi
    issues, in social dreaming matrix, 125, 137
creativity, 164, 165
    and blindness, 11
    and social dreaming, 40
    use of, 177–178
Crossan, J. D., 117, 119
culture(s):
    change, conditions for, 111–112, 115
    characteristics of, 108
    corporate, and shared experience of members, 107–121

Daniel, P., xviii, 17, 85, 142
Davis, S. M., 110
day residues, dreams as, 35
Deal, T. E., 107
Delta Consulting Group, 108
De Mare, P., 112
Deming, W. E., 108, 112
democracy, 109, 115
DePaul University, Chicago, 117
dialogue(s), 19, 23, 33, 40, 45, 91–106, 144
    context for, 91–106
    on-line, 143
    seating arrangement for, 92
dichotomies, in Western mind, 172–173

discovery vs. invention, 10–11
displacement, and dreaming, 2
dream(s), *passim*
　and action, 4
　anxiety-, of falling, 38
　as container for meaning, 105
　Australian Aborigine, 25–27,
　　139
　as biological necessity, 2
　censor, 28, 32
　connectedness in, 30
　as container of meaning, 105
　cryptic or hidden meaning of,
　　30
　as day residues, 35
　and everyday activities, 36–39
　expression, by Senoi, 37
　German, 23–25
　　pre–World War II, 15–17
　as guardian of sleep, 27
　as hero-journeys, 31
　image and reality, link between,
　　xviii
　interpretation, by Senoi, 37–39
　interpretation of, 2–3, 60, 105,
　　139, 164
　　vs. associating to, 164
　Israeli, 20–23
　as link between finite and
　　infinite, 127
　material, sequencing of, xx
　multifaceted meanings of, 35
　as "Other", xx
　as parables, 119, 142
　parables as, 116–121
　as puzzles, 30
　as recycling of past, 51
　scientific analysis of, 2
　as source of information, 118,
　　169
　as source of revelation, 44, 50
　in systems-centred theory, 59–68
　thought processes in, 4
　and transformations, 101

　vs. visions, 50
　as wish-fulfillment, 27
　-work, 8, 28, 149
　　failure of, 7
　　and thinking, 5
dreaming:
　central to evolution, 2, 3, 39
　as contextual process, 2
　and creativity, 38
　lucid, 14
Dreamtime (Australian Aborigine
　　myth), 26, 139
Dyer, W. G., 110

Edison, T., 146
educational setting, use of social
　　dreaming in, 4, 43–48
Einstein, A., 6, 181
Eisold, K., 4, 49–58, 67
Emerson, C., 76
Emery, F., 110
Emery, M., 110
emotional experience:
　boundaries of, 101
　and capacity to dream, xxi, 2
　of group, 101
　mental space as container for,
　　xx
　primary, nature of, 100, 101
　space of, 101
　system-in-mind, 101
　and transformation, 100–102
Euclidean space, 6, 170, 171
evolution:
　cultural, in organizations, 110
　process of, dreaming central to,
　　2, 3, 39
evolutionary biology, 110

finite and infinite, dream as link
　　between, 2, 127
flight to change, 99
fortune-telling, dream as, xviii, 13
free-association, 1, 4, 8

Freud, S., 2, 11, 27, 28, 30, 32, 105,
    139
Freudian psychoanalysis, 142
Fromm, E., 28

General Motors, 174
Gestalt therapy, 116
Gillespie, G., 35
Glacier Metal Works, 109
Gleick, J., 114
Goethe, J. W. von, 133
Gore, A., 111
Gould, L., 52, 55, 56, 124
group:
    capacity of for play, 47
    vs. matrix, 4
Grubb Institute, The, 91
Guisiano, D., 128

Hahn, H., 4, 43–48
Hall, E. T., 111–113, 119
hallucination, of leadership, 8
Hart, A. W., 113, 114
Hirschhorn, L., 114
Hitler, A., 16
Hobson, J. A., 179
holding environment, group as, 56
Holloway, J., 29
Horton, D., 44

imagery, interplay of, xx
imaginal life:
    of individual, 171
    of organization, 127
imaginal space, 170
IMAGO East-West, 92
Indian Society of Applied
    Behavioural Studies, 1
Indians, British Columbian, use of
    dreams by, 36, 40
industrial society, 170, 171, 172
inertia, vs. change, 99
infinite, the, 1, 127, 170–173, 178,
    181

and dreams, 3, 9–41, 170
and finite, dream as link
    between, 2, 127, 170
information:
    dreams as source of, 169
    society, 172
    and organizations, 179
    technology, growth of, 178
Innovation and Change in Society
    (Israel), 19
innovation(s), originating in
    dream, 181
Institute for Intercultural
    Psychodynamic Research,
    92
Intensive Journal Workshops, 31
International Foundation for
    Social Innovation, Paris, 18
interpretation:
    of dreams, 2–3, 60, 105, 139, 164
    vs. association, 164
    of emotional experience,
        100–103
    in management of
        transformation, 99
    multi-dimensional, 175
invention vs. discovery, 10–11
irrationality of organization, 110
isomorphy, 67

Jacob's Ladder, 39
    dream, 34
Jaques, E., 109, 142
journey-dreams, 10, 47, 53, 55, 80,
    88, 130, 133
Jung, C. G., 9, 27, 30, 69, 70, 71
    vision of Europe's future of,
        14–15
    theory of, 20, 31, 142

Kalahari, people of, use of dreams
    by, 13
Keats, J., 73
Kekulé von Stradonitz, F. A., 181

Kelly, A., 76
Kennedy, A. A., 107
Kennedy, J. F., 57
Kets de Vries, M., 110
King, A., 19
King Lear, 81, 83–90
King, M. L., 68
Klein, E., 67
Kleinian psychoanalysis, 142
Kraft, C., 110
Krantz, J., 151, 161

La Fontaine, J. de, 133
Lasch, C., 28
Lawrence, W. G., xvii, xviii, xix,
        xxi, 7, 9–41, 46, 51–52, 58,
        60, 81, 85, 89, 91–93, 103,
        116, 119, 123–140, 142–144,
        166, 169–181
leadership, 8, 113, 149
    and organizational culture, 110
Lewin, K., 109, 110
Lifton, R. J., 12, 39
linear thinking, 4, 6

Maltz, M., 4, 6, 141–167, 169–181
Mandelbrot set, 10
matrix:
    social dreaming, *see* social
        dreaming matrix
    use of term, xviii, 17
    as ziggurat, 34
McCulloch, W. S., 98
McGregor, D., 109
McLuhan, M., 60
Meier, C. A., 2
Meltzer, D., 27, 28, 30
memory:
    and desire, 11
    of lost childhood, 79
mental space, 106
    boundaries of, xx
    definition, xx

and dream, xx, 3
    as communication from or
        into, xx
    of matrix, 136
Menzies, I. E. P., 142
metaphors and dreams, 2, 4, 75–90
Michael, T. A., 4, 59–68, 107–121,
    142
Miller, D., 110
Mills, C. W., 126
Milton, J., 11, 170
mind, psychoanalytic theories of,
    32
minicultures, 112
Mitchison, N., 17
Moore's Law, 176, 178
Morgan, H., 4, 69–73
Morson, G., 76
Mountford, C. P., 26
mutual consultation sets, 19, 23, 92
myth, 26, 105, 118–120
    vs. parable, 117
    world-creating, 118

narcissism, 172
negative capability, 73
New York University, 142
Newton, I., 6
nihilism, 172
no-dream, 4, 8
Noschis, K., 71

"O" [Bion], 41
Oedipus, 5, 58
Oeser, F., 4, 75–90
Ogawa, 14
oneiromancy, 13
open systems theory, 50
openness, 4, 105, 115
optical space, 170, 171, 172
organization(s), *passim*
    adaptibility of, 177
    changing nature of, 175–176

as contained, 176
creativity of, 177–178
destructiveness of, 177–178
and information, 178
-in-the-mind, 102
multidimensionality of, 175
simplicity/complexity of,
    174–175
thinking of, 178–179
Organizational Development
    Network of Greater New
    York, 146
organizational life:
    emergent quality of, 6
    as it is dreamt, 6
    as process, 5
    role of dreaming in, 4
    see also corporate culture;
        organization
organizational settings and
    boundaries, 102

parable:
    as apologue, 120
    as dream, 116–121
    dream as, 119, 142
    vs. myth, 117, 119
    and politics of salvation, 119
    social dreams as, 118
Paramatman, 1
patterning, xx
Penrose, R., 10, 11
Peters, T., 107, 108, 109
Piper, R., 112
Plato, 98
politics of revelation, 44, 119, 127,
    142
    vs. politics of salvation, 60, 119,
        127
Praxis Event, 137
Presley, E., 146
primary apprehensive self and
    secondary comprehensive

self, communication
    between, 65
primitive Christians, use of
    dreams by, 119
primitive peoples, dream theories
    of, xviii, 13, 14, 35, 38
process consulting, 109
profound knowledge, system of,
    108
Progoff, I., 31
projective identification, 100, 143
prophecy, dream as, xviii
psychoanalysis, use of dreams in,
    2
psychodynamics of organizational
    culture, 65, 109
psychosis, 138
    of unconscious social processes,
        137
    socially induced, 127

quantum mechanics, 1, 110
quantum physics, 172–173
    and causation, 171

Radcliffe-Brown, A. R., 35
randomness of environment, 6
rational madness, 126, 127
    of organizations, 138
reality as continuum of particles
    and waves, 171
Reed, B., 91
relatedness, 29, 34, 87, 91, 101–102,
    175
    definition, xvii
    man–cosmos, 41
    within organizations, 102
    in social dreaming matrix, 76
relativism, 172
rescue phantasy, 127
resistance:
    to change, 149
    to transformation, 99

resonance, 62, 65, 66
revelation:
    through dreams and
        associations, 75
    politics of, 44, 60, 127, 142
        vs. politics of salvation, 60,
            119, 127
    and social dreaming, 41
Rice, A. K., 53, 104
    Institute, 52, 119
Roberts, A., 26

Saint-Denys, Marquis de, 14
salvation, politics of, 44, 119, 127
Savary, L. M., 128
Schein, E. H., 108, 109
search conferences, 110, 112, 115
seating arrangement:
    circular, of group, as container,
        66
    for dialogues, 92
    in social dreaming matrix, 17,
        20, 31, 32, 46, 66, 70, 81
secondary comprehensive self and
        primary apprehensive self,
        communication between,
        65
Seiler, D., 40
Senoi, 40
    social cooperation of, 37–38
sequencing, of dream material,
    xx
Shakespeare, W., 4, 76, 81
    King Lear, 83–90
Shell International Petroleum
        Company, 5, 18, 177
Shephard, H., 109
Sievers, B., 24
Smith, Kline & Beecham, 107
social analysis, application of, to
        corporate culture, 109
social climate, effect of social
        dreaming on, 4, 69–73

social dreaming, passim
    concept of, 1
    definition, xvii
    future of, 39–41
    origins of, xvii–xix, 13–18,
        27–30, 125–128
    primary task of, 18, 30–31
    working hypotheses on,
        136–140
social dreaming matrix, xix, xxi, 8,
        10, 41, 51, 69, 138, 180
    in Australia, 25–27
    boundaries for, 164
    and change, concept of, 31–33,
    containing capacity of, xix, 21
    development of, 17–20
    and environment, 29
    experimenting with, 44–48
    in France, 126–136
    in Germany, 23–25
    vs. group, 4
    in Israel, 19–23, 36–37
    multi-verse of meanings in, 31
    on-line, 141–167
    as prism, 23
    seating arrangement in, 17, 20,
        31–32, 46, 66, 70, 81
    shades of biographies in, 32
    in Switzerland (at International
        Congress), 69–73
    in United Kingdom, 18, 44–48,
        75–90, 92–94
    in United States, 32, 52–58, 61–
        68, 116–117, 120–121, 141–
        167
social dreams as parables, 118
social processes, unconscious,
        psychosis of, 137
society:
    industrial, in Euclidean space,
        171
    information, 170–181
        vs. industrial, 170

space:
    acoustic, 6, 170–172
    -infinite, 170
    Euclidean, 6, 170, 171
    imaginal, 170
    mental, *see* mental space
    optical, 170, 171, 172
spirit, good or bad, access to,
        dream as, xviii
splitting, in psychotic thinking, 7
Stewart, K., 37, 38
Storr, A., 11, 12
story:
    creation of, with dreams, 130
    myth as, 117
    parable as, 117, 118
    use of as founding myth, 118
structuralist analysis, 117
subjectivism, 172
Summerson, J., 80
Sutton, P., 26
symbiont collaboration, 181
symbiont relationships, 129
symbiont techniques, 179
Symington, J., 170
Symington, N., 170
systemic consultation sets, 92
systems:
    and boundaries, 102
    -centred theory, 59–68
    theory, open, 50
    thinking, 110

Taiwanese, fortune-telling through
        dreams by, 13–14
Tannen, D., 112
Tatham, P., 4, 69–73
Tavistock:
    Centre, xviii, xix, 142
    Institute of Human Relations,
        17, 109, 123
        Group Relations Programme,
            xvii, 18, 142

"technology", 139
terrorism, as theme in action
        research group, 52–58
thinking:
    creative vs. linear, 6
    and dreaming, 4
    kinds of, 94–98
    linear, 4, 6
    psychotic, 7
    vs. thought, 94–98
    and transformations, 96–98
Third Man, The, 78–83
Thompson, S., 112
thoughts vs. thinking, 94–98
Tibetan Yogis, use of dreams by, 14
Tiplitz, M., 36
Tolstoi, L., 75
Total Quality Management (TQM),
        108, 112
transference, 17, 28, 33, 143
    as context of dream, xxi
    dynamics, in groups, 44
    issues, in social dreaming
        matrix, 21–23, 70, 125, 134,
        137
transformation:
    vs. change, 98–102
    holistic, 76
    management of, 44, 99–100, 106
travel-dreams, *see* journey-dreams
Triad Consulting Group LLC, 151,
        152
Trice, H. M., 108
Trist, E., 110
Trotsky, L., 98
Turquet, P., 103

Ullman, M., 29, 39, 169, 180
Unamuno, M. de, 139, 171
unconscious, the, 2, 16, 24,
        123–125
    and dreams, 39, 127, 139
    as gift from, 13

unconscious, the (*continued*)
  of groups, 143
  role of, in organizational
    consultation, 164
  as source of dreams, 40
University of Kent, 104
unpredictability of environment,
    6
unthought known, 60, 126, 127,
    135, 179–181
Upanishads, 1

Van der Post, L., 13, 34
vision:
  vs. dream, 50
  dream as, xviii
  role of, in organizational life, 4,
    49–58

Walker, E. M., 4, 6, 141–167,
    169–181
Warner, L., 109
water, theme of, in dreams, 13, 15,
    80, 129, 132–133, 137
Waterman, R. H., 108, 109
Weisbord, M. R., 110, 115
Wendt, H. A., 107
Wheatley, M. J., 110, 111
White, K., 52
Whitehead, A. N., 170
William Alanson White Institute
    (WAWI), 55, 125
  Organizational Development
    and Consultation
    Programme, 52, 143, 146,
    164
Wink, W., 116, 117
Winnicott, D., 105
wish-fulfilment, dream as, 27
Wittgenstein, L. von, 96
Worledge, N., 104

Yeats, W. B., 101
Young, R., xx, 3

Zohar, D., 173